Dedicated to my mother
and Sam

Out Law

Other books in the Queer Action/Queer Ideas series

Come Out and Win, by Sue Hyde

Out Law

What LGBT Youth
Should Know about
Their Legal Rights

Lisa Keen

Queer Action/Queer Ideas,
a series edited by Michael Bronski

Beacon Press, Boston

BEACON PRESS
25 Beacon Street
Boston, Massachusetts 02108-2892
www.beacon.org

Beacon Press books
are published under the auspices of
the Unitarian Universalist Association of Congregations.

10 09 08 07   8 7 6 5 4 3 2 1

This book is printed on acid-free paper that meets the uncoated paper
ANSI/NISO specifications for permanence as revised in 1992.

Composition by Wilsted & Taylor Publishing Services

Library of Congress Cataloging-in-Publication Data

Keen, Lisa.
    Out law : what LGBT youth should know about their legal rights / Lisa Keen. — 1st ed.
        p. cm. — (Queer action)
    ISBN-13: 978-0-8070-7966-9 (hardcover : alk. paper)
    ISBN-10: 0-8070-7966-9 (hardcover : alk. paper) 1. Gay youth—Legal status, laws,
etc.—United States—Juvenile literature. I. Title.

    KF4754.5.Z9K44 2007
    342.7308′772—dc22   006031583

Contents

Appendixes

A Note from the Series Editor

It is no surprise that Lisa Keen's book is unique—indeed, it's literally the first of its kind. The fact is that *Out Law* could not have been written thirty, or even fifteen, years ago. The idea that young lesbian and gay people should know about the laws specifically affecting them is a new one. It is an idea that has grown out of LGBT youth activism since the 1980s, and the enormous changes that have occurred in high schools with the growth of gay-straight alliances and support groups run by students.

Laws are important in our society, yet these laws can be unfair and cruel to young people, as well as to other groups. Historically, young people have been told that they will be protected by their families, their elders, and their government. This happens far less than it should, and so it is imperative that young LGBT people learn to take care of themselves.

Lisa Keen's comprehensive look at what LGBT young people need to know about the law—how the law affects them specifically, how their lives can be changed (for the better and/or worse) by the law, and how they can work with the law to make their lives safer, healthier, and more productive—is a crucial and empowering step in transforming the reality of young LGBT lives.

MICHAEL BRONSKI
Series Editor

Foreword
Kevin Jennings

Lisa Keen's book took me back to my teaching days and made me wish that I had this wonderful resource then. While its obvious target audiences are LGBT youth and their allies and advocates, the former history teacher in me wished I'd had it ten years ago to use as the basis for my civics lessons, as Ms. Keen provides an easy-to-understand guide to our legal system and how it works. It takes a truly gifted writer to explain in plain language how laws get made and enforced, and the fact that Ms. Keen has done this so well (without charging $350 an hour) speaks to her skill as a writer and thinker.

Unfortunately this wonderful book cannot serve solely as a text for school lessons. In fact, it may prove to be something of a survival guide for LGBT students, the vast majority of whom face routine harassment while at school (nearly 75 percent, accordingly to the 2005 *National School Climate Survey* conducted by the Gay, Lesbian, & Straight Education Network [GLSEN]). In the ideal world, school staff would do something about this, but in the real world, they usually don't: according to the GLSEN survey, most students (58 percent) don't even bother to tell teachers when harassment occurs, because they don't expect much will change if they do—with good reason, as only 16 percent of LGBT students who witnessed staff intervention in incidents of harassment said that this intervention was "very effective" in dealing with the problem (over half said it was completely or somewhat ineffective). Sadly, LGBT students simply cannot count on school staff to "do the right thing."

In a world where sexual-minority youth face routine harassment and school staff do little to stop it, a guide such as this will prove invaluable to LGBT students, their parents, and their allies. It's natural to feel a little hopeless and a little helpless when you're subject to injustice and the authorities do nothing about it (and, as shown in this book, sometimes it's the authorities themselves who are the source of the injustice). But Lisa Keen helps LGBT students understand that they do not have to be victims but can use the law to fight back. If school staff won't do the right thing, they can be forced to do so through appropriate use of the law. That's a lesson every LGBT student, their families, and their allies need to learn.

Preface

You may have committed a crime.

That's right. If you had sexual relations with a person of the same sex prior to 2003, you may have committed a crime. Maybe even a felony. Prior to June 26, 2003, when the U.S. Supreme Court ruled that the Constitution protects an individual's right to have sex with a person of the same sex, having same-sex sexual relations was a crime in many states.

But that ruling doesn't necessarily get you off the hook. If you have sex with a person of the same sex who's under the age of sixteen, you might still be committing a crime. It all depends on how old you are and where you live.

The legal and political landscape for openly lesbian, gay, bisexual, and transgender people has definitely improved in recent years, but the law is still very much a factor in our lives.

As this book was being written, the United States Congress, for the second time in two years, was debating a bill to take away many of our rights because we're lesbian, gay, bisexual, or transgender. Courts in California were preparing to decide whether we can have children. And right-wing legal groups were pressing lawsuits and ballot measures around the country in hopes of winning a legal right to discriminate against us.

That's the big picture. Up close, it gets more personal.

If you are a young person in school, chances are you frequently hear other students call you or somebody else "gay" as a put-down. Unlike everybody else in your class, you may be harassed or even disciplined by school officials for showing affection to a boyfriend or girlfriend. You may be told that you have to get a permission slip from your parents to take your date to the prom. And you may be afraid to wear your favorite pride T-shirt for fear of getting beat up.

Under these conditions, it's hard not to feel picked on. But there are laws that can provide you with some defense. The catch is this: You have to know about those laws and you have to defend those laws against erosion by people who want to discriminate against you.

Knowing how to defend your rights as a citizen is not just a matter of self-defense and self-interest. There's more at stake than whether we, as sexual minorities, are able to secure our rights as citizens. Below the surface of these skirmishes over "gay rights" is a struggle to control the culture and direction of America. The outcome of that struggle will define the parameters of what it means to live in a democracy. And that has consequences for everybody.

Caveat

ca-ve-at. *n.* 1a. A warning or caution: *"A final caveat: Most experts feel that clients get unsatisfactory results when they don't specify clearly what they want"* (Savvy). b. A qualification or explanation.
—*The American Heritage Dictionary of the English Language*

This book is not a substitute for professional legal advice from an attorney. It is important to remember that every person's legal dilemma—no matter how common it may seem—involves a unique person, a distinct set of facts, and a specific jurisdiction. A solution that might work today for a twenty-year-old in California who is already out to family, friends, and coworkers may be totally inappropriate tomorrow for a fifteen-year-old in North Carolina who has never self-identified as gay.

What this book *can* do is help you understand that, wherever you are, you have rights, and you have options for protecting yourself and your rights. There are many options beyond filing a lawsuit, and sometimes those options can remedy a bad situation more quickly and easily than taking the matter before a judge. But sometimes legal action is called for, and having an attorney on your team becomes an imperative.

If you find yourself in a situation in which legal action is necessary to protect yourself or your rights, Appendix F at the back of this book will give you some places to start in finding appropriate legal advice or counsel.

1

It's Your Fight

A high school student in Missouri wore a T-shirt to school one day that carried the message "I'm gay and proud." His homeroom teacher sent him to the principal's office, and the assistant principal told him that some students might find the message offensive. The official told the student to either turn the shirt inside out so the wording could not be seen or go home and change. If that happened to you, what would you have done?

At a high school in California, a girl gave her girlfriend a kiss and hug, like other girls would give to their boyfriends. But in this case, the principal suspended the girl from school and called her parents to tell them—without her permission—that she was gay. How would your parents have reacted?

A physical education teacher at another high school in California learned that one of her students was a lesbian. She barred the student from attending her gym class. Would you know where to turn for help if this happened to you?

In Nevada, some students forcibly put a lasso around an openly gay student's neck and threatened to drag him from behind a truck. School officials responded not by punishing the attackers but by transferring the gay student to a school for troubled youth. What would school officials in your town have done?

And at a high school in Florida, when a female student chose to wear pants and a suit jacket instead of a feminine low-scooped shoulder drape for her senior portrait, the principal ordered a yearbook editor to omit the photograph from the annual. Would you have given in and worn what they told you to wear?

Law Degree Not Required

Given the enormous advances of the gay civil rights movement in recent years, one might guess that these events occurred in the 1950s or 1960s. But they all happened in just the last few years. Similar incidents are taking place in all parts of the country. In each case, young people had their legal rights trampled on. But with the help of a lawyer, each of these individuals fought back to protect those rights, with some measure of success.

But how do you know when your rights are being violated? Sometimes school officials and other authorities have a right to tell you what you can and cannot do. Sometimes they have a legal *obligation* to talk to your parents about your personal life. What can be done to stop someone from calling you names or attacking you?

The answers to many of these questions are matters of law, but it doesn't always take a lawyer to figure out what your rights are and how to protect them. And while you may not need a lawyer, you need the law and you need to know enough about the law to know when to say, "You can't do that. I have rights." And then, if somebody violates your rights anyway, you need to know how to go about getting help to make them stop.

Generally speaking, the rights of young persons are the same as those of adult citizens of the United States. Some rights are guaranteed by the U.S. Constitution to every citizen; some are matters of federal law but apply only in certain circumstances.

But some of a young person's rights can be legally curbed. If you're under twenty-five years of age, car rental companies can deny you the right to rent a car or they can charge you more than they do older drivers. If you're under twenty-one, most bars and restaurants can't sell you an alcoholic beverage. And until you're eighteen, you can't vote in federal elections.

Age limits on other rights can vary by state.

The "age of majority" is a legal term that defines the age at which you can legally be considered an adult and when you become responsible for most, if not all, of the decisions regarding your life. That age is eighteen in all but four states. (In Alabama and Nebraska it is nineteen; in Mississippi and Pennsylvania it is twenty-one.)[1] Prior to reaching this age, you are, legally speaking, considered an "unemancipated minor," and your parents or guardians have a legal responsibility to take care of you—to feed you, clothe you, give you shelter, and see that you receive necessary medical care.

In most cases, once you reach the age of majority you are "emancipated." That means you are automatically deemed to be an adult and can enter into legal contracts, manage your own property, consent to medical treatment, join the military without your parents' consent, and file a lawsuit.

It is possible for you to become an "emancipated minor"—assume legal adulthood sooner than your state's age of majority. This has two major impacts: It gives you the right to be treated as an adult before you reach the age of majority as defined in your state of residence, and it releases your parents or guardians from their legal responsibility to take care of you and make decisions for you. One way to achieve this status is to get married—assuming you meet state-defined age requirements for marriage. Another way is to petition the court to declare your emancipation. Requirements for these petitions differ from state to state. California, for instance, requires that you be at least fourteen years old, fill out a form showing your living expenses and means of support (a legal source of income), and persuade the court that you are willingly choosing to separate from your parents or guardians and that you have either their "consent or acquiescence" to this decision.[2]

And in case you've ever thought of running away from home, you should know that you could be subject to arrest in some states and that —if you're under the age of twenty-one—your parents can get police help in finding you.[3]

Interestingly, war has had a significant influence on the legal definition of adulthood. According to the Close Up Foundation, a non-profit citizenship-education organization, the logic behind considering twenty-one as the age of adulthood dates back as far as the eleventh century, when it was believed that a man was not strong enough to wear armor until that age.[4] In the United States in the early 1970s, the voting age was lowered to eighteen nationwide because males were being drafted as young as age eighteen to serve the U.S. military in Vietnam. Proponents argued that if you were old enough to fight and die for your country, you were old enough to vote.

The Purpose of Law

Most of us trust that the authority figures in our lives—school officials, police officers, parents—are justified to tell us things like, "You can't do this" or, "I'm going to make you do that." But adults are human and they can't know everything; they don't know every law, and they won't always know how to help you.

Unless you're an exceptionally wealthy and resourceful young person, you can't whip out your cell phone and call a lawyer every time someone calls you a "faggot." And in fact there may not be a legal response to every trespass against you as a lesbian, gay, bisexual, or transgender (LGBT) person.[5] But there *are* times when actions and words directed at you—because, as an LGBT person, you are part of a sexual minority— pose a serious enough threat or have serious enough consequences that you *must* act.[6] Your knowledge of the law can be a powerful weapon in your arsenal of defense.

As complicated as it can get, on one level law is simple: It's a rulebook. When you live with other human beings, there have to be rules. At home, these are probably unwritten: "If you're not coming straight home after school, call me and let me know where you are." Or, "No foul language in front of your little sister." Or, "No television until after dinner." These kinds of rules protect you and your family members. And they create an environment that makes it possible for several people to share limited space and resources.

The same is true for towns and states and countries, except the rulebook is much more formal and complex. As fellow citizens we share much more than a bathroom and two televisions. As a country, we share land, water, air, and schools. We pool our energies and money to build highways, hospitals, and cable lines.

Laws are created to help us live together peacefully, share our mutual resources fairly, and make sure we don't kill one another over the last available parking space at the shopping mall. The rules are as complicated as the tax code and as easy as knowing on which side of the road we're supposed to drive.

When it comes to making laws, different groups of people— whether they constitute nations, states, or cities—have different opinions about what is civil and what is fair, and so their laws can be different. In the United States, most of us believe that all people should be treated as equals; but in some countries, many people believe that men are superior to women (a belief generally held by men, in male-dominated societies in which women's views are held to be unimportant). In the United States, women and men are treated equally under the law; in Ukraine, Moldova, Nigeria, the Dominican Republic, Burma, and Thailand, women can be bought and sold.[7]

In the United States, the law protects the right of each citizen to worship through whatever religion he or she chooses, while in Saudi Arabia, the law requires that each citizen be a Muslim.[8]

Many laws directed toward young people in the United States were created to protect youth from abuse and exploitation. These include laws that attempt to stop the sexual abuse of children by defining the age at which an individual can legally consent to sex. Other laws protect minorities and groups subject to victimization, such as laws aimed at stopping hate-motivated assaults by allowing courts to inflict harsher punishments for crimes motivated by hatred toward a particular group, such as LGBT people.

It's Not All about Protection

But not all laws that affect sexual-minority youth are aimed at protecting you. Some create obstacles for you and for other young people who want to explore their sexual identities. In 1996, for instance, Congress passed a law to prohibit the sending or displaying of "patently offensive" messages over the Internet in a manner that would make such messages available to a person under eighteen years of age. It also prohibited the transmission of obscene or indecent messages to any recipient younger than eighteen.[9] The U.S. Supreme Court struck down the laws the following year, noting, among other things, that they could stifle a serious discussion about homosexuality and other controversial topics.[10]

Even straight people can be affected by laws that are aimed at helping or obstructing LGBT people. Straight students can be misidentified as gay, lesbian, bisexual, and transgender—whether accidentally or on purpose—and be subjected to the same kind of harassment. And if the local library blocks out Internet searches that include the word "sex," the computer blocks them out for everybody.

While the three-letter word "sex" seems to stand out in many people's minds whenever discussions revolve around LGBT people, for many young people, sex—including sex with a person of the same sex—is one part of a natural and significant search for self. And in that search, some young people find themselves experiencing attractions toward people of the same sex. Those who do may find themselves wondering, "Am I gay or is this just a phase?" Confronting questions about love and attraction is part of growing up, and answering them is part of the process of developing character.

Fortunately, for a growing number of people, it is no longer considered healthy to run away from such tough questions or to hide from answers that might identify you as a sexual minority. Today, there is greater acceptance of sexual-minority youth among young people and that growing acceptance provides you with a greater level of security in being open about who you are.

Nevertheless, greater openness toward sexual difference among youth still runs up against an older, less accepting part of society—a part that still controls many positions of authority. In some cases, that authority is parents, teachers, and principals. In other cases, it is those who make and enforce laws at the local, state, and federal levels.

Figuring out whether your sexual attractions are to people of the same sex is one thing. Deciding whether to act on them is another, and like your straight friends, many LGBT young people could benefit from advice from a safe source. Straight youth often find this safe source in school. Sex education courses cover such topics as how to avoid pregnancy and sexually transmitted diseases. But those kinds of courses are geared almost exclusively toward heterosexual sex. Relatively few provide any information about the how-tos and what-not-to-dos of same-sex sexual activity. And asking a question about homosexuality in class could feel intimidating or embarrassing for many sexual-minority youth.

Once you come out as an LGBT person, you know you will be treated differently, but whether you come out or not, your sexual orientation will affect your relationships with your family, your friends, and others. It will probably factor into what college you want to go to, whether you will join the military, and where you choose to live. In some places, laws make these decisions easier, and in some places, more difficult.

It's Just One Difference

Every young person faces difficulties. Some have trouble making good grades. Others have a physical disability. Some perceive themselves to be too big or too small. Some feel unattractive. Others feel pressure to keep up with their parents' expectations of success. Many have problems at home—an alcoholic parent, an abusive sibling, or even an eating disorder or drug addiction.

The difficulty you face as a young lesbian, gay man, bisexual, or transgender person is similar in some ways to the difficulties that other young people face. The difference can cause emotional pain and worry, and it distracts you from concentrating on school, work, and enjoying life.

For some youth in some places, being LGBT may not cause much hardship. Some communities welcome diversity and have safeguards in place to make sure that every young person is treated with dignity and respect.

In other places, hostile attitudes toward sexual minorities can drive a young person to drop out of school, run away from home, or engage in self-destructive behaviors.

But It's a Powerful Difference

A professional polling firm surveyed 3,450 students ages thirteen to eighteen and 1,011 secondary school teachers from around the country in 2005. Its findings, contained in *From Teasing to Torment: School Climate in America, A Survey of Students and Teachers,*[11] demonstrated that a majority of students (65 percent) were harassed for some reason—their race, sexual orientation, or disability, just to name a few. Thirty-nine percent were harassed because of some aspect of their physical appearance. One-third of students were harassed because they were gay or because someone perceived them to be gay.

Sixty-nine percent of students said they frequently heard phrases such as "You're so gay" or "That's so gay" as a put-down of another student. Fifty-two percent reported frequently hearing fellow students make homophobic remarks.

Beyond the matter of how individual LGBT youth experience their sexual-minority status, there are outside factors that have a positive or negative impact on that experience. For instance, when prominent individuals or celebrities—such as Ellen DeGeneres and Elton John—publicly acknowledge being gay, the general public's familiarity with sexual-minority status is increased. That often increases the public's comfort level when encountering ordinary LGBT people. Similarly, when public figures express negative sentiments toward gays—such as when a majority of senators in Congress support an antigay law—public sentiment often hardens against sexual minorities, creating an environment where some people feel it's OK to harass or attack LGBT people.

Lambda Legal Defense and Education Fund, a national gay-civil-rights group, reported seeing a dramatic increase in hostilities directed at sexual-minority youth in late 2004—a spike the organization attributed to the widespread debate around same-sex marriage generated by the presidential campaign.

"We're alarmed by a noticeable increase in gay youth facing discrimination or hostility in just the last month since the election," said Michael Adams, director of education and public affairs at Lambda in December 2004.[12] That election—which in November 2004 led to a second term for Republican president George W. Bush—put an unprecedented amount of focus on LGBT people and issues. The campaign media focused frequently on the perceived differences between the two major-party candidates on the issue of gay marriage, and many states had measures on their ballots asking the public to ban same-sex marriage in their states. While the surface issue was marriage, the subtext was whether gay people deserve the same rights as other U.S. citizens.

Lambda found that many jurisdictions were not ensuring that LGBT youth had the same rights as others. For instance, near the end of 2004, a high school in Utah instituted a new requirement that any student wanting to take a same-sex date to a school dance had to first get written permission from their parents. Written parental permission was not required to take a different-sex date.

"The rights of gay youth are very clear," said Lambda's Adams, adding that they should not be "up for public debate."[13]

Fear of Fighting Back

But such rights may not always be clear to *you* or to those who have a responsibility to protect you. Many sexual-minority youth do not know what their rights are or how to assert them. One national survey documenting the experiences of LGBT students in schools found that, although most schools had antiharassment policies, four out of five did not mention anti-LGBT harassment.[14]

Another survey, *Hatred in the Hallways,* found that many LGBT students spend "an inordinate amount of time plotting how to get safely to and from school, how to avoid the hallways when other students are present so they won't be slammed into lockers, how to cut physical education class to escape being beaten up—in short, how to become invisible so they will not be verbally and physically attacked by their peers.... Exacerbating the abuse from peers is the failure of adults to protect them."[15]

Regardless of whether an individual school or school district has a policy to discourage harassment, sexual-minority youth, like all Americans, should be protected by the U.S. Constitution's guarantee of freedom of expression and equal protection. And yet there have been numerous reports of school officials refusing to allow students to wear T-shirts with gay-pride messages. Sexual-minority youth, like all Americans, should have the freedom of association, yet some librarians have been required to use content-filtering software that can obstruct students' Internet access to research into LGBT-related science and sociology. Federal laws ensure that groups, including LGBT groups, can meet on an equal basis with other groups, yet parents can wield veto power over what clubs their children belong to and who they take to a school dance.

Many LGBT youth have fought back against these injustices and many are winning. As you'll see later in this book, the student who wanted to wear his gay-pride T-shirt to school eventually dropped out of school, but his initial efforts to fight the antigay policy inspired other students who were able to change it. The girl who refused to wear the ultrafeminine drape for her senior portrait forced the school to change its policy, too. The girl who was transferred out of her school because she hugged and kissed her girlfriend was able to return to her original high school to finish her senior year. The student assaulted by classmates who tied a lasso around his neck and threatened to drag him from the back of a truck won a large monetary settlement plus agreements by his school district to change its policies for handling harassment and to train its faculty to better respond. And the student who was thrown out of gym class because she is a lesbian is fighting that decision in court. Just by fighting back, each of these young people has contributed to a better world for others. The key to their success has been in recognizing when their rights had been violated and defending those rights through the law.

2

You're a Sex Symbol

You'll often hear older LGBT people say that things are easier today for young people—that society is more tolerant, there are more laws to protect you from discrimination, and it's easier to meet other LGBT people than it was twenty or thirty years ago. Even though there's a lot of truth to those views, some things *haven't* changed.

Now, as in years past, the general public tends to see the difference between *homo*sexual and *hetero*sexual as *sexual*. Scientifically speaking, the difference is only in the choice of sexual partner. If you're homosexual, you have sex with a partner of the same sex (*homo*),[1] and if you're heterosexual, you have sex with a partner of the other sex (*hetero*).[2]

Whenever the word "sex" enters a discussion, everyone's attention seems to orbit around it. Even when you try to keep the focus on things such as discrimination and equal rights for "gay people" and "lesbians," your efforts can be undermined by an unspoken fascination and fear of the sexual mystery that LGBT people conjure up for many people.

For most people, this fascination or fear is fleeting, and once they get past it, they are able to see LGBT people as ordinary at worst, fabulous at best, but certainly of no threat to them or anyone else.

Yet some people stay mesmerized by that difference. Perhaps as a way to explain the intensity of their interest in LGBT people, they conjure up the idea that we pose a danger—like witches and demons—and claim that we must be fought. And of course they volunteer for duty.

There is little doubt that, for some people, the expression of hatred toward any group is an effort to cover up feelings of curiosity or attraction to that group—feelings that the person is uncomfortable with and is desperately afraid will be revealed. For others, it's the result of an inability to cope with the unfamiliar or fear of the unknown. And certainly for some, it's a modeled behavior, something learned from an important figure in a person's life—a parent, a priest, or some other role model. Kids aren't born loving baseball; they learn to love it from the people around them. And they learn to hate that way too. So we won't always understand *why* a particular person hates gay people, or hates all LGBT people, we just know that some people do.

And we also know that more young people today seem to be accepting of LGBT people. A national survey of one thousand fifteen-to-twenty-five-year-olds in the United States found that almost nine out of ten believe there should be laws protecting "homosexuals" from discrimination; six out of ten would approve legal recognition of same-sex relationships.[3]

For most young people today, curiosity about anything sexual is just a natural part of growing up and figuring out who they are. "Do I like girls?" "Do I like guys?" "Do I like girls *and* guys?" "Am I gay?" "Is my curiosity just a phase or will it last?"

Sometimes, to find the answers to those questions, you might feel like you want to have sex with somebody to see if you like it; sometimes, you won't. Everybody is different and every day can be different. Things that might "feel right" and safe on one day with one person might not feel the same on another day, in another place, or with someone else.

Some people explore through doing; others prefer to think things through before trying something for the first time. And some people make decisions based on a wide variety of concerns and values—from "safe sex" considerations to peer pressure and family and religious beliefs.

No matter how *you* approach sexual exploration and learning about who you are, you're going to go through something that everyone goes through.

Most people ultimately find that their feelings and attractions are drawn to partners of the other sex. A relatively small minority are drawn to partners of the same sex. An even smaller minority find themselves drawn to both sexes. For some, the exploration involves considering a change in their own physical gender. And, though people seldom talk about it, some people never have sex.[4]

But if you explore by *doing*, one thing has definitely gotten easier in recent years. Having sexual relations with a same-sex partner is no longer illegal. Until the U.S. Supreme Court decision in *Lawrence v. Texas* in 2003, same-sex sexual relations were crimes in many states.[5] There are still laws that criminalize sex based on the ages of the participants, but those laws—age-of-consent laws—are now pretty much the same for straights and sexual minorities in every state.[6]

How Many Make a Minority?

If you're an LGBT young person, you've probably wondered how many other people around you, in school or at a party or a concert, are like you. Maybe you wonder how many other people want to start a gay-straight alliance, or how many are having the same problems as you with a teacher who says derisive things about LGBT people.

You've probably heard the commonly voiced statistic that 10 percent of people are "gay."

There is some truth to that figure, but just as human beings can be more complicated than a simple "gay or straight" answer, the statistics around how many people are part of this minority are also complicated. Attempts to nail down a reliable number to reflect what part of the general population in the United States is lesbian, gay, bisexual, or transgender are often made difficult by cultural and legal restrictions around asking personal questions, particularly when it comes to surveying young people.

And statistics that have been gathered vary a lot depending on how you word the question, what population you're surveying, and how comfortable a person feels in responding honestly.

Just look at the terms "homosexuality," "bisexuality," and "heterosexuality." A heterosexual is someone who has sex with a person of the other sex, right?

What if the person hasn't had sex with anyone yet? Where will you count him or her? Should a man be labeled "homosexual" if only once, as a teenager, he had a brief sexual encounter with a same-sex friend? Should a woman be categorized as bisexual if she has had sex with two men and one woman but has been exclusively with the woman for the past five years?

There's no rulebook on how to apply these labels in the real world, so each survey taker defines his or her own rules. And while professional surveys very often explain how they interpret information, the media, in reporting the results, don't always spell that out.

The results of surveys on sexuality also vary considerably depending on what population is being studied. If you survey one thousand people in rural Utah, you'll probably find a rather tiny percentage of people willing to identify as "gay." That's because Utah has an unusually high percentage of Mormons, members of the Church of Jesus Christ of Latter-day Saints, which considers sexual relations between persons of the same sex to be immoral. But it's also because rural populations are small, and small groups of people tend to bond around common values and needs. Finding another LGBT person in a tiny population is likely to be difficult, and that's why many LGBT people move to cities.

If you conduct a study in a large metropolitan area, the percentage of people identifying as "gay" is likely to be relatively large. That's because large populations tend to value and welcome diversity, often protect minorities from discrimination through various laws, and provide a multitude of ways in which gay people can find one another to form communities and relationships.

A study conducted by the National Center for Health Statistics in 2002 found that the percentage of people in metropolitan areas who had had a same-sex partner in the previous twelve months was more than twice that of people in "nonmetropolitan" areas.[7]

And of course, survey results can vary widely depending on the age group of the study population. Studies of adults in their twenties, thirties, and forties will almost certainly find a larger percentage of people identifying as "gay" or acknowledging a sexual experience with a person of the same sex, as compared with studies of teenagers younger than sixteen. Under age sixteen, most teens have not yet had a heterosexual experience.[8]

OK, But What About "10 Percent"?

For years, the gay community and others believed that "gays" comprised about 10 percent of the population. No one is entirely sure where that number came from, but one of the more plausible explanations is that it was derived from data from the first scientific studies of homosexuality.

Scientific studies published in the United States by Dr. Alfred Kinsey in the late 1940s and 1950s reported that 37 percent of 5,300 men studied had engaged in sexual activity with a same-sex partner at least once in their lifetimes. *Ten percent* were predominantly homosexual for at least three years between the ages of sixteen and fifty-five. And 4 percent were exclusively homosexual as adults. Kinsey's study of 5,940 women found that 13 percent had engaged in sex with a same-sex partner at least once in their lifetimes, 28 percent acknowledged having engaged in "covert or overt" homosexual activity; and about 2 percent were exclusively homosexual as adults.[9]

Today, experts believe that slightly less than 10 percent is more accurate, at least when looking at the general population nationally.

"I think the consensus is that somewhere between 3 and 6 percent of the population identifies as nonheterosexual," says Dr. Charlotte Patterson, a researcher in the field of sexual orientation and professor of psychology at the University of Virginia.[10]

"Nonheterosexual"? Most transgender people identify with the gay civil rights movement because they experience discrimination in many of the same ways as homosexuals and bisexuals, but most identify themselves as heterosexual.[11] That puts them in the majority when it comes to sexual orientation.

"Their intrinsic difference," according to "A Primer by Transgender Nation," "is their gender identity"—or how they appear to the world.[12] In a U.S. Centers for Disease Control study conducted in 2002, about 90 percent of people between the ages of eighteen and forty-four surveyed identified as heterosexual.[13] That would seem to leave 10 percent as LGBT, right?

Not exactly. First you have to look at how many people did *not* answer the questions. Then you have to look at what the questions were. In this study, unlike many others, the survey asked questions about sexual activity, identification, and attraction.

Looking at *self-identification*, 1.8 percent of people surveyed simply would not answer the question, "Do you think of yourself as heterosexual, homosexual, bisexual or something else?" Might their numbers be added to the LGBT numbers, or were they just uncomfortable with answering such a personal question? We don't know. But of those who answered the question:

- 90 percent of men and women said "heterosexual";
- 2.3 percent of men and 1.3 percent of women said "homosexual";
- 1.8 percent of men and 2.8 percent of women said "bisexual";
- 3.9 percent of men and 3.8 percent of women said "something else."

When asked about with whom they actually *had sex,* the percentages were much higher. They were also much more complicated and varied significantly by age and sex. For instance, among fifteen-to-seventeen-year-olds, 13 percent of males and 11 percent of females had engaged in oral sex with a partner of the other sex but not vaginal intercourse. With older age groups, the likelihood that a person had engaged in both oral and vaginal intercourse increased. Looking at the entire fifteen-to-forty-four-year-old survey group:

- 6 percent of men had had either oral or anal sex with another man at some time in their lives, 2.9 percent had had a male sexual part-

ner in the previous twelve months, and 1.6 percent had had *only* male partners in the previous twelve months;
- 11 percent of women had had some kind of "sexual experience" with another female at some time in their lives,[14] 4.4 percent had had a female partner in the previous twelve months, and 1.3 percent had had *only* female partners in the previous twelve months;
- 1 percent of men and 3 percent of women had had sex with both a male and a female partner in the previous twelve months;[15]
- 10 percent of men and 8 percent of women had never had sex with anyone.

But among fifteen-to-nineteen-year-olds, 4.5 percent of men and 10.6 percent of women had had sexual contact with a person of the same sex at some time in their lives, and 2.4 percent of men and 7.7 percent of women had had such contact within the previous twelve months. Among twenty-to-twenty-four-year-olds, 5.5 percent of men and 14.2 percent of women had had sexual contact with a person of the same sex at some time in their lives, and 3 percent of men and 5.8 percent of women had had such contact within the previous twelve months.

This survey also asked people questions about *sexual attraction.* Among eighteen-to-forty-four-year-olds:

- 92 percent of men and 86 percent of women were attracted only to the other sex;
- 3.9 percent of men and 10 percent of women were attracted "mostly" to people of the other sex;
- 3.2 percent of men and 3.4 percent of women were attracted only, "mostly," or equally to partners of the same sex.

Deciding for Yourself

It's important to keep in mind that there is no legal requirement that you identify yourself in any of these categories. And just because you identify yourself to friends as "gay" or "straight" today does not mean that you have to stick with that label for life.

Having sex with a person of the same sex does not make you gay, and having sex with a person of the other sex does not make you straight. You are who you are. And hopefully, your world is friendly enough and safe enough that you feel free to be honest about that.

And though it's rarely discussed, there's a difference between being "gay" and being "homosexual"—a difference that many people—even people in the LGBT community—often lose track of.

Referring to a person as a "homosexual" these days presumably means that the person has sexual partners of the same sex. Like "heterosexual," the term refers to only *one aspect* of a person—the sex of his or her sexual partner.

Generally speaking, the word "gay," in modern usage, refers to more than the sex of a person's sexual partner. It can describe someone who has never had sex with a person of the same sex. "Gay" most often is used to describe a person who is attracted to same-sex partners and is *willing to be identified* as part of a community of other people with attractions to same-sex partners.

Research has demonstrated that a person's attraction to partners of the same sex is largely based in genetics.[16] But the decision to publicly identify as gay is a personal decision you make for yourself. Some people do; some do not. It is possible for a person to have homosexual attractions and to engage in sex only with persons of the same sex and never identify as "gay."

Since the very early days of the gay civil rights movement, gay political organizations have been plagued with the problem of people's reluctance to identify themselves as LGBT. In the 1980s, numerous surveys showed that only about 20 percent of the people who considered themselves to be "gay" acknowledged that fact in most arenas of their lives.

That percentage is almost certainly higher today, given the more welcoming climate that has evolved over the years. While there are difficulties and negative consequences to identifying as gay even today, it is no longer considered psychologically healthy to hide one's homosexuality. And in today's world, the greater acceptance of sexual-minority youth by their peers provides LGBT youth with a greater sense of safety and comfort in deciding to be honest about matters of sexuality and identity.

3

The Evolution of Difference

Many aspects of our culture are rooted in the societies of long ago. For instance, shaking hands is a custom that is believed to have originated in medieval times, as a gesture of peace between two knights to demonstrate that neither was carrying a weapon. A menu's offering of fish on Friday is rooted in the traditional practice of some Catholics to abstain from eating red meat on Fridays. The expectation that a man would take the curb side when strolling with a woman came from a time when streets were not paved and a passing carriage frequently splattered mud on pedestrians. Wearing a wedding ring on the third finger of the left hand comes from an ancient belief that "love's vein" ran from the heart to this finger and that the ring would prevent love's loss.

Nowadays, people do not always greet each other with a handshake, some menus offer only red meat on Fridays, men do not routinely take the curb side when walking with a woman, and though many married people wear wedding rings, few if any believe that their feelings of love for their spouse will escape if they take the ring off to wash their hands.

Similarly, few people understand how homosexuality came to be treated so differently from heterosexuality. Some will point to passages in a Bible to justify negative feelings and opinions about homosexuality. But those texts have been open to individual interpretation for centuries, and the same people who point to passages that they believe admonish homosexuality ignore passages that ban activities commonly accepted today, such as eating shellfish or pork. And even those who say their hostility to homosexuality is based on a strict reading of the Bible are able to ignore passages that condone such practices as slavery.[1]

Many of the customs and attitudes society holds today are based on ancient beliefs that have—over the centuries—been rejected or proven wrong.

The origin of how treating people who engage in sex with a partner of the same sex came to be seen as "different" is a fascinating tale—one that began as an effort to address what was seen as a threat to the human race, then became a political power struggle and, ultimately, a scientific quest.

To begin with, it's important to remember that society in general feels more comfortable with conformity than it does with difference. It's human nature: Everyone is more comfortable with what they know than with what they don't know.

People in a minority—any minority—experience a sense of being different, whether what distinguishes them is relatively invisible—such as being left-handed—or striking—such as being dark-skinned in a community where most of the people are light-skinned. Often, people in the majority do things that make those who are different feel inferior.

It Hasn't Always Been "Different"

For most of recorded history, sexual relations between same-sex partners were hardly seen as different at all. When they had sex, most people engaged in heterosexual relations, but people were not separated by labels of "heterosexual" or "homosexual," "gay," "lesbian," "bisexual," "straight," or "transgender." People were humans who engaged in sex, usually with a partner of the other sex but sometimes with a partner of the same sex. Neither the words nor the concepts of "homosexuality" or being "gay" or "lesbian," "bisexual" or "transgender" existed.

In 1980 John Boswell, a Yale professor and gay historian and researcher, wrote that sexual relations between males occupied a prominent and respected position in ancient Greece and Rome and other Western cultures.[2]

"As late as the eleventh and twelfth centuries, there appears to be no conflict between a Christian life and homosexuality," Boswell said. "Gay life is everywhere in the art, poetry, music, history, et cetera, of the eleventh and twelfth centuries. The most popular literature of the day, even heterosexual literature, is about same-sex lovers of one sort or another."[3]

These ancient societies did not think of sexuality as being either homosexual or heterosexual. Sex was sex, regardless of the sex of the parties involved.

In most of these societies, same-sex sexual relations were completely accepted.[4] But to some extent, this acceptance was conditioned on the expectation that a man would have sex only with a person of lower societal status than himself, that is, a woman, a slave, or a younger male. In such sexual relationships, the individual with the higher social status was expected to be the dominant partner. And when a boy became an adult, he was expected to no longer accept a passive role in sex.

"To continue in a submissive role even while one should be an equal citizen was considered troubling," wrote the political philosophy scholar Brent Pickett. Still, Pickett argued, there is evidence of "many" adult sexual relationships between men at the time, including many that were "not strongly stigmatized."

"Greek gods, such as Zeus, had stories of same-sex exploits attributed to them, as did other key figures in Greek myth and literature, such as Achilles and Hercules," Pickett stated.[5]

The Greek philosopher Plato felt that love could be earthly in nature, and beget children, or be heavenly and beget "offspring of the soul." (This is the origin of the term "platonic love"—which in today's terms means love that does not involve sex.)

Sex: Everybody's "Sin"

Historians have shown that negative attitudes toward what we know today as homosexuality originated with Christian church leaders, who didn't just pick on homosexual sex. They had a negative attitude toward *any* kind of sex.

Popular belief, back then, was that "good" things are based in nature (hence the term "natural law"). It was this type of thinking that led to interpretations of biblical stories (such as the tale of Sodom and Go-morrah—hence the word "sodomy") which held that *nonprocreative sex outside of marriage* was against nature.

While the word "sodomy" today is associated most frequently with sexual acts between same-sex partners, traditionally it meant *any* sexual act that was *not for procreation*. This included same-sex sexual relations, masturbation, oral sex, anal sex, bestiality, "and [for Christians] even sexual intercourse with Jews and [Muslims]," according to the Dutch historian Theo van der Meer.[6]

This attitude of the Church—that nonprocreative sex or sex outside of marriage was bad—was eventually written into law, when the first civil law code was set down under the Christian Roman emperor Justinian I. Those laws, in 529 CE, influenced other societies in other centuries as they put together their own legal codes.

The negative attitude began to focus more exclusively on homosexuality in the twelfth to fifteenth centuries, in part because the bubonic plague was causing a precipitous drop in population in certain parts of Europe. One Italian religious leader, Bernardino of Siena, reportedly railed against nonprocreative sex in the 1400s after the plague caused a drop in the population of Florence from 120,000 to 40,000. Men who spent their "seed" in nonprocreative sex were seen as jeopardizing the survival of the people.

Over time, the "sin" and "crime" of engaging in nonprocreative sex or homosexuality was punished with whipping, imprisonment, exile, or worse. In Spain, during the Inquisition of the 1500s, "sodomites" were burned at the stake. In the Netherlands during the 1600s, they were strangled to death. In France in the 1700s, they were burned at the stake or exiled to colonies an ocean away (including in the New World).[7]

In England in the sixteenth century, Henry VIII broke away from the Catholic Church but retained most of its laws. And the laws of the American colonies, settled by the English and other Europeans, were based on Old World laws. As more states entered the Union, they, too, included laws against sodomy in their criminal codes.

From Sin to Sickness

Scientific knowledge enabled people to move beyond the belief that the world was flat, and it eventually affected attitudes about homosexuality too. As early as the 1700s, science advanced society's knowledge about nature and began to exercise greater influence over people's attitudes. It also began to usurp some of the Church's authority to define what was "natural."

By 1869, medical science had begun to explore the matter of sexual relations between people of the same gender. In doing so, it found evidence suggesting that the tendency of a person to choose a same-sex sexual partner was based in their nature, just as choosing a partner of the other sex was natural for most people.

On the positive side, people began to protest harsh punishments for individuals who engaged in nonprocreative sex outside of marriage. Laws prohibiting sodomy began to be used selectively, primarily in prosecuting cases involving rape or sex with minors.

But on the negative side, people also began to consider same-sex sexual activity as a medical issue or illness.

There are conflicting accounts of the origin of the word "homosexual," though there is general agreement that it emerged in the latter half of the nineteenth century in the context of discussions about finding the cause for same-sex sexual activity and attraction. Interestingly, there was no parallel search for the origins of heterosexual activity and attraction, but by the early 1900s, medical scientists believed that they had narrowed down the cause of homosexuality to some *defect* in the biology or environment of the persons who engaged in such activities.

The nineteenth-century German sexologist Richard von Krafft-Ebing suggested that homosexuality was a hereditary disease caused by the domination of the wrong brain center. Sigmund Freud, the founder of psychoanalysis, saw it not as a physical defect but one of environment. In his "Letter to an American Mother" in 1935, Freud reassured a mother who had a homosexual son that homosexuality "cannot be classified as an illness; we consider it to be a variation of the sexual function produced by a certain arrest of sexual development."[8]

This new notion—that homosexuality was some form of medical disorder—did not entirely supplant the old notion that homosexuality was a sin. Even today, some people cling to that view; but it is a view based on their interpretation of the Bible, not science or law. Nor is there any real concern today that the population of this country or another might be jeopardized by a huge majority of people abandoning heterosexual activity and procreation. And the Kinsey research published in the late 1940s and 1950s had provided a stunning blow to the centuries-old myth that homosexuality was a rare and freakish phenomenon.

The Evolution of Variation

As medical science continued to study people who engaged in homosexual activity, more and more information was uncovered supporting the understanding that homosexuality was a *biological variation*.

In 1955, perhaps influenced by Kinsey's findings, the American Law Institute proposed a Model Penal Code, which omitted laws prohibiting consensual sodomy.[9] The first state to adopt the model was Illinois. Its legislature, in revising the state's criminal code, became the first state body to eliminate its own law prohibiting sodomy, in 1961.

Meanwhile, the American psychologist Evelyn Hooker, in the late 1950s and 1960s, was preparing to deliver a knockout punch to the idea that homosexuality was a freakish defect. Hooker's studies revealed that people who engaged in same-sex sexual relations were not suffering from a disorder but very often leading ordinary, happy, and well-adjusted lives. As head of a Task Force on Homosexuality formed by the National Institute of Mental Health (part of the National Institutes of Health), Hooker issued a report stating that there were "at least three or four million adults in the United States who are predominantly homosexual and many more individuals [in] whose lives homosexual tendencies or behavior play a significant role."

The Hooker Report recommended that the government "remove legal penalties against acts in private among consenting adults."[10] The administration of then-president Richard Nixon suppressed the report, according to one task force member, Dr. John Money. The report had been submitted to the Nixon administration—in October 1969—at a particularly critical moment in the political evolution of gay people. Starting with a riot by gays against police who were raiding a gay bar called Stonewall in New York City on June 27, 1969, gay people around the country were becoming more open about their homosexuality with the public at large. Rather than accept the medical label of "homosexual," they insisted on being defined as "gay."

The following year, a gay publication in California obtained a copy of the Hooker Report and published it, and gay activists began pressing for its general release. In 1971, the government did print the report and the medical community was given further evidence to contradict the idea that homosexuality was an illness. In the face of the Kinsey and Hooker studies, the American Psychiatric Association (APA) in 1973 began to reclassify homosexuality and remove any suggestion that it constitutes a disorder.[11]

"Science was saying it's not a problem," said June Reinisch, a former director of the Kinsey Institute, "so more people in the general population could believe it's not a problem."[12]

Modernizing the View of Law

The growing understanding of same-sex sexual orientation fueled the determination of many gay people to fight discriminatory treatment by police and others. Gay political activists began seeking the adoption of local laws to prohibit discrimination based on sexual orientation. And that push forward by gays was met by a push back by some who argued that their religious beliefs required them to actively oppose treating gay people equally.

So while twenty-two other states had joined Illinois in adopting the American Law Institute's model code by the early 1970s, and in doing so eliminated their sodomy laws,[13] some states chose to narrow their sodomy laws to apply only to sex between partners of the same sex.[14] Many attempts were made to strike down these laws, and more than a dozen lawsuits were appealed to the U.S. Supreme Court. In 1976, in *Doe v. Commonwealth,* two gay men from Richmond, Virginia, challenged that state's sodomy law, arguing that it violated their rights under the U.S. Constitution, including the right to privacy, freedom of expression, and due process, and constituted cruel and unusual punishment.[15] The Supreme Court upheld their conviction without comment.

Ten years later, twenty-four states and the District of Columbia still had such laws on the books. Most of them prohibited "sodomy" by anyone—including heterosexual couples—but they were seldom enforced against anyone other than LGBT people.[16]

In 1986, a gay man from Georgia, Michael Hardwick, asked the U.S. Supreme Court to strike down his state's law against sodomy. Hardwick had been having sex with a man in the bedroom of his apartment when a police officer walked in on them—reportedly to serve Hardwick with a warrant for failure to appear in court on an unrelated misdemeanor charge. The officer arrested both men, but only Hardwick sought to challenge the law.

The Supreme Court rejected Hardwick's request to strike down the state sodomy laws, saying that the right to privacy implicitly guaranteed by the U.S. Constitution protected only *fundamental* rights, such as marriage and procreation. Sex between "homosexuals," said the Court, even in the privacy of their own homes, could not possibly be considered fundamental. Writing for the five justices who formed the majority opinion, Justice Byron White said that protecting the right of gay people to have sex in the privacy of their own homes would be like protecting illegal drug use, incest, adultery, "and other sexual crimes even though they are committed in the home."

Furthermore, said the majority, laws prohibiting sodomy had ancient roots. The Court simply did not address the fact that those ancient roots also proscribed other forms of nonprocreative sex. Instead, noted the opinion filed by the four justices dissenting from the majority view, the majority "distorted" the questions raised by the law to simply ignore its application to heterosexuals.

The 1986 *Bowers v. Hardwick* decision marked an enormous setback for the gay civil rights movement.[17] While police rarely had opportunities to discover gays having sex in the privacy of their bedrooms, the existence of the law still meant that such activity was illegal and that, if you were having sex with a same-sex partner, you were violating a law. Anyone who acknowledged being "gay" in those twenty-four states and the District of Columbia was, in essence, acknowledging that they violated or had a propensity to violate the law. And in some states, breaking that law was considered a felony. So in saying that you were "gay" you could also be identifying yourself as a felon.

Sodomy laws, then, enabled employers, landlords, and others who wanted to discriminate against gay people to do so simply by arguing that such individuals were criminals.

The devastation of the *Hardwick* decision prompted gay legal activists to rethink their efforts to repeal sodomy laws. As long as the majority of the Supreme Court justices were resistant to seeing gay people the same as other citizens, there was no reason to take a case to that court.

"Given the reasoning and the tone of the majority opinion, as well as the increasingly conservative and political posture of the [Supreme] Court," wrote Abby Rubenfeld, managing attorney for Lambda Legal Defense and Education Fund in 1986, "it would be foolhardy to pursue" another sodomy repeal case "at this time."[18]

Despite the enormity of the setback, gay legal activists did have some success in repealing sodomy laws on a state-by-state basis. In 1992, for instance, the Kentucky Supreme Court struck down that state's sodomy law, saying that the state's constitution does "offer greater protection of the right of privacy than provided by the Federal constitution as interpreted by the United States Supreme Court." The Kentucky high court ruled that the sodomy statute violated that right to privacy and the state constitution's guarantee of equal protection.[19]

At the same time, gay political activists were having increasing success persuading local governments to adopt laws prohibiting discrimination based on sexual orientation. As they succeeded, antigay political activists escalated their efforts to repeal such laws.

By the early 1990s, right-wing religious activists were on the offensive, trying to persuade voters to pass laws to *legalize discrimination* against gays. Through a number of local, state, and national conservative religious groups, antigay operatives devised a plan to put initiatives on the ballot in a number of states that would not only repeal any existing laws to prohibit discrimination based on sexual orientation but would amend state constitutions to legalize such discrimination. To sell the idea to voters, the proponents argued that laws prohibiting discrimination based on sexual orientation amounted to "special rights" for gay people.

It made sense. "Gay rights" sounds like something only gay people can have. But despite the popular use of the term "gay rights," there really was no such thing. What people in the LGBT community were seeking, in passage of nondiscrimination laws, was not a *special right* to do something or have something that no one else could have. They were seeking an *equal right* to be treated like everyone else, and to prohibit employers, landlords, and others doing business in the public arena from treating them with bias.

One of the first of the antigay initiatives to pass was Amendment 2 in Colorado in November 1992. Gay legal activists challenged the initiative in court and won. But the State of Colorado appealed the decision and, finding no support in the state courts, eventually took its appeal to the U.S. Supreme Court.

By the time the state's appeal of *Romer v. Evans* reached the U.S. Supreme Court in 1995,[20] the makeup of the high court bench was very different from what it had been in 1986. Six justices had since left the bench, including three of the original five who had formed the majority in *Hardwick*.

On May 20, 1996, the Supreme Court issued its ruling in a 6 to 3 decision: the antigay ballot measure was unconstitutional. In an opinion written by one of the Court's newer justices, Anthony Kennedy, the majority said Amendment 2 violated the U.S. Constitution's guarantee that all citizens have equal protection of the law. It also ruled that the state had no rational reason for treating gay people differently from others and that Amendment 2 was a reflection of society's "animus"—or hostility—toward gay people.

"We must conclude that Amendment 2 classifies homosexuals not to further a proper legislative end but to make them unequal to everyone else," wrote Justice Kennedy for the majority. "This Colorado cannot do. A state cannot so deem a class of persons a stranger to its laws."

The ruling in *Romer v. Evans* was an enormous victory for gay activists seeking equal rights, and it set the groundwork for the repeal of all state sodomy laws—through the *Lawrence v. Texas* decision in 2003.

But despite these successes, the negative attitudes toward LGBT people have persisted, and other laws reflect a lingering reluctance to treat LGBT people the same as heterosexuals. Many Americans oppose the idea of same-sex couples being able to marry. Openly gay people are still essentially barred from serving in the military.

Young LGBT people, like their straight counterparts, are not likely to investigate the origins and intentions of laws regarding sexual activity. But understanding why having a same-sex partner has carried such a stigma for so long can help you dispel any myths that might be lingering in your own mind about why we are treated so differently. It can also help in circumstances in which others are spreading misinformation—either deliberately or inadvertently. In this way, LGBT people are always on the front lines in the battle against bigotry.

4
The Least You Need to Know

Imagine this: You're sitting in a car with a friend. It's nighttime, and the car's parked in front of a store that's closed. You've just been to a party where you've had some beer, but now you're just two guys (or two girls) sitting in a car, talking. Suddenly, a police car pulls up behind you with its lights flashing. The police smell alcohol on your breath; you're both under twenty-one, so they decide to arrest you for underage drinking. While frisking your friend, the police find a condom, which they decide is evidence that you're both "queer" and must have been planning to have sex in the car. On the way to the police station, one of the officers says he knows your family and that he's going to tell them that you're gay. You've never told anyone you're gay and you know your family will react negatively to this news. What do you do?

There's no easy answer to this question. And there's not just one correct answer. But this is a real-life dilemma that confronted one young man in Pennsylvania in 1997. His response was a tragic one.

Marcus Wayman was eighteen and living with his grandfather in the small Pennsylvania community of Minersville. His parents had moved to Texas for work reasons, but Marcus wanted to finish up his senior year in high school, where he was on the football team. Just a month before graduation he had gone to a football party, and afterward he was giving a male friend a ride home. But instead of going directly home, they parked in the empty parking lot of a local store that was closed for the night. Police noticed the car and, knowing the store had recently been burglarized, pulled up behind it to investigate.

In the course of questioning Marcus and his friend, who was seventeen at the time, police determined that they had been drinking and began arrest procedures. While frisking them, police found two condoms in the friend's pocket. One of the police officers accused the two young men of being "queers" who were parked there in order to have sex. While sex between same-sex partners was still illegal in some states in 1997, it was not illegal in Pennsylvania. But the officer lectured the young men about the Bible's condemnation of homosexuality, and he told Marcus that he knew his grandfather and that he was going to tell him that Marcus was gay.

Marcus feared that his grandfather would be repulsed by this allegation, and that he would throw the teenager out of the house. Distraught, he went home and wrote a note to his grandfather, saying that he did not want "everyone's life [to] be ruined by mine." He then shot himself in the head, ending his life.

Marcus's sexual orientation is not known. He never told anybody he was gay. But whether he was gay or not doesn't matter. He was horribly injured by the fact that somebody threatened to tell other people that he was gay and he didn't feel that there was anything he could do about it.

His mother filed a lawsuit against the police officers, and years later a federal appeals court ruled that the actions of the officer who made the threat violated rights guaranteed to every citizen under the U.S. Constitution. According to a decision by a federal court, "matters of personal intimacy," including information about a person's sexual orientation, are "protected from threats of disclosure by the right to privacy."[1]

If he had known this, maybe Marcus could have used this information to silence the police officer's threats. Maybe not. But it's important to know that laws exist to discourage inappropriate behavior on the part of public officers. It's also important to understand that not every LGBT person in a situation similar to Marcus's would necessarily have the same constitutional protection. How could that be? A metaphor might help.

Singing the Law

Think of law as music in its written form. Different performers interpret the written music in different ways. One performer might sing a song in a lively, upbeat manner, and another might render it in a slower, more solemn way. So it is with courts in their interpretation of the law.

In its written text, the U.S. Constitution does not say anything *explicitly* about a "right to privacy." However, over the past several decades, the U.S. Supreme Court has ruled that it does *implicitly* guarantee a right to privacy in a number of matters. For instance, in 1965, it ruled that "specific guarantees in the Bill of Rights have penumbras."[2]

The Bill of Rights, the first ten amendments to the Constitution, includes such guarantees as the freedom of speech and religion, and the freedom of association. A "penumbra" is a transition zone between one distinct area and another—such as between light and dark. In this transition zone, things are neither light nor dark but somewhere in between. In legal matters, the term "penumbra" is often used to describe where *implicit rights* exist—they are not explicit in the text but they are not absent either.

After the U.S. Supreme Court ruled that a right to privacy is implied in the Constitution, it began—in subsequent cases—to define how much of a person's life that right protected. Among the things it covers, said the Court, are a couple's decision about whether to use contraceptives,[3] and "personal rights that can be deemed 'fundamental' or 'implicit in the concept of ordered liberty.' "[4]

In ruling on the lawsuit brought by Marcus's mother, the U.S. Court of Appeals for the Third Circuit noted that the U.S. Supreme Court also ruled, in 1977, that the constitutional right to privacy "respects not only an individual's autonomy in intimate matters, but also an individual's interest in avoiding divulgence of highly personal information."[5] Information about Marcus's sexual orientation "was an intimate aspect of his personality entitled to privacy protection," said the Third Circuit, and the Minersville police had no good reason to threaten to divulge that information to Marcus's grandfather. (In some circumstances, the government can violate a person's constitutional rights but it must be able to convince the court that it has a good reason to do so.)

In our country's federal court system, decisions by the U.S. Supreme Court affect everyone on a nationwide basis. But if a decision comes from a lower court, it affects only the geographical area of that court. Thus, the Third Circuit's opinion that information about a person's sexual orientation is protected by the Constitution applies only to states and regions in the Third Circuit—Pennsylvania, New Jersey, Delaware, and the U.S. Virgin Islands. As the Third Circuit noted, one other circuit has issued a similar ruling concerning transsexualism, and three other circuits have issued similar rulings concerning information about a person's sexual experiences and about a minor's "personal sexual matters."[6]

But the Fourth Circuit has ruled that the right to privacy does not protect information about whether you have had sex with a person of the same sex.[7] So if you live in Maryland, North Carolina, South Carolina, Virginia, and West Virginia, you may be more vulnerable to this type of threat.

One thing to keep in mind, however, is that interpretations of the law change. When the Fourth Circuit issued its ruling that there was no privacy protection for information about a person's sexual orientation, the prevailing interpretation of the Constitution was also that *nothing* in the Constitution protected an individual's right to have sex with a partner of the same sex. That, as you'll read about in the next chapter, is no longer the case.

5

It's Alive!

When most of us think about the U.S. Constitution, we think of the rights that have been associated with this nation's identity since its very beginning—freedom of speech, freedom of religion, and the right to associate with whomever we want. But what most people forget from their high school history lessons is that these most precious rights were *not* part of the original U.S. Constitution. These rights, and others, were added as amendments to the Constitution after it was signed. The first ten—which helped lay the groundwork for the right to privacy—are known as the Bill of Rights.

In high school, studying the Constitution—amendments and all—can be a big yawner. Most of the text makes for quite drab reading:

> We the People of the United States, in order to form a more perfect union, establish justice, insure domestic tranquility, provide for the common defence . . .

> The supreme court shall have appellate jurisdiction, both as to law and fact, with such exceptions, and under such regulations as the Congress shall make.

> Full faith and credit shall be given in each state to the public acts, records, and judicial proceedings of every other state. . . .

> The Congress, whenever two-thirds of both houses shall deem it necessary, shall propose amendments to this constitution, or, on the application of the legislatures of two-thirds of the several states, shall call a convention for proposing amendments, which, in either

case, shall be valid to all intents and purposes, as part of this constitution, when ratified by the legislatures of three-fourths of the several states....

Too boring! Right?

Consider this: Each one of these plodding excerpts has, or will very soon have, direct impact on your life as an LGBT person.

While you may have managed quite nicely up to this point without whipping out your copy of the Constitution in defense of your life, people who oppose equal rights for LGBT people are wielding their copies with increasing frequency. Many right-wing conservative political organizations are, for instance, arguing that judges who interpret the Constitution in a way that treats LGBT people as equal citizens are trying to "usurp democratic legislative authority."[1] Although it has failed twice in the U.S. Senate, a proposal to amend the Constitution to prevent judges from interpreting it as protecting the relationships of LGBT people as it does those of straights is almost certainly to return in future Congresses. And the 2004 Republican Party platform called for using Article III of the Constitution to designate the anti-LGBT Defense of Marriage Act as being outside the jurisdiction of courts.

Article III—that's the part that says that "the supreme court shall have appellate jurisdiction, both as to law and fact, *with such exceptions, and under such regulations as the Congress shall make.*"

Given that Republicans held the White House and a majority of seats in both houses of Congress, these ideas are more than idle threats for LGBT people. To stop them from becoming realities, LGBT people, like you, have to fight back. And to fight back, you need to know what you're fighting for.

Your Rights Are Not "Special"

Although right-wing opponents of equal rights for LGBT people have always been fond of claiming that LGBT people seek "special rights," the

LGBT political movement has, in fact, been focused squarely on securing only those rights promised by the Constitution to all citizens. As discussed earlier, there is no such thing as "gay rights" or "LGBT rights." There are *constitutional* rights, and they are the same for all people and should belong to all citizens.

Today, it's LGBT people fighting to defend and preserve the Constitution, but through the years, it has been many other groups of citizens —African Americans, women, immigrants, people with disabilities, and others.

During the Civil War, citizens of this country fought one another over whether the rights and freedoms promised by the Constitution could be denied to people born in this country but whose ancestors had been forcibly taken from their native lands and enslaved. Contrary to popular belief, that fight didn't end with the Civil War; it continued even *after* the war, but eventually, we added more amendments to the Constitution to abolish slavery and guarantee that, regardless of race, every adult male citizen would have all the rights of citizenship, including the right to vote.[2]

Through the course of various other political movements, other amendments have been added, including one to extend the vote to women and one to extend the vote to citizens between the ages of eighteen and twenty-one.

The fact that certain groups of citizens have needed specific amendments in order to enjoy the guarantees of the Constitution illustrates the dynamic relationship between the centuries-old document and the sentiments of its current population. It was only because American society grew to see the lives of women as worthy of the same respect as the lives of men that the Nineteenth Amendment was ratified in 1920 to ensure that women could vote. It was because the country was drafting eighteen-year-old men to fight the war in Vietnam that the Twenty-Sixth Amendment was ratified in 1971 to ensure that citizens who had reached the age of eighteen could vote.

Today, American society wrestles with its feelings about LGBT people, and some members of the U.S. Congress are trying to amend the federal constitution to limit the rights of citizens who are not straight. It's hard to predict whether they will be successful, but ensuring the equal rights of *all citizens* will depend on our willingness to stand up for the Constitution and protect the promise made in its Preamble—"to secure the blessings of liberty to ourselves and our posterity."

The Limits on Liberty

There is no set definition of what is meant by "the blessings of liberty." Different scholars have suggested different things—for instance, the rights granted through the Bill of Rights, or the "unalienable rights" referred to in the Declaration of Independence, which include "Life, Liberty and the Pursuit of Happiness." And, as the woman's suffragist Susan B. Anthony observed, the Preamble states that the Constitution is to "secure" these rights, not *grant* them.[3]

Securing these rights can get a little tricky, especially for young people. There are limits on people's rights to freedom of speech and other constitutional rights. For example, the government can stop you from exercising such rights if what you're doing or saying endangers the lives or the rights of other citizens.

For instance, a person can't go into a crowded bar and shout "Fire!" as an exercise of free speech. To do so could trigger a stampede that could lead to injuries and death. A person can't threaten to harm or kill you by claiming that his religious beliefs call for the eradication of homosexuality.

As young people, you have greater need for the Constitution's protection. You are more likely to challenge views that have been long held by the majority, probably more willing to voice your opinions in public, and certainly more apt to see the world with a fresh perspective.

But as young people, you do not enjoy all the protections and guarantees of the Constitution that other citizens enjoy. As already discussed, if you're younger than eighteen, you can't vote. Your liberty can be restricted by your parents or legal guardians. And the right to privacy that most citizens depend on can be curtailed for you by school officials who have an obligation to inform your parents about certain issues.

As a minority, LGBT people have more impetus to fight for the Constitution than others because our differences can put us at odds with the majority, and the majority wields power through the size of its voting bloc.

6

Law
The Mother of All Arts

You may have already learned this the hard way, and you've certainly been hearing about it in this book: Despite all the talk about the Constitution guaranteeing equal rights for all citizens, all citizens do not have equal rights. Especially not you.

As mentioned in Chapter 1, if you're younger than twenty-five, car rental companies can charge you more or can refuse to rent to you, even if you've never had an accident or a traffic violation.[1] Until you're twenty-one, federal law denies you the right to buy or publicly possess alcoholic beverages.[2] If you're under eighteen, you can't buy a lottery ticket and you can't legally make medical-treatment decisions for yourself.[3] And if you're LGBT, just try getting a marriage license outside Massachusetts, adopting a child inside Florida, or joining the military anywhere in the United States.

In the case of young people, much of the disparate treatment can be explained by a desire to protect youth from their own inexperience and impetuosity, though some of the motivation is to protect insurance companies, car rental agencies, and others from the documented frequency of youthful mishaps.

But there is no documented justification for treating LGBT people differently under the law. In passing the federal "Don't Ask, Don't Tell" law in 1993, essentially barring openly gay people from serving in the military, Congress justified the exclusion by saying that gay people posed "an unacceptable risk to the armed forces' high standards of morale, good order and discipline, and unit cohesion."[4] Yet not one military unit has been identified as having suffered "morale" issues because of the presence of a gay person and, instead, military studies going back as far as the 1950s provide no evidence to support those justifications.[5] In passing the federal Defense of Marriage Act in 1996, Congress claimed it was attempting to "protect the institution of marriage."[6] Yet no member of Congress offered one example of a marriage that had been destroyed because of a marriage license being issued to a same-sex couple. And the reason behind banning gays from adopting in Florida was explicitly stated as a desire to have gay people "go back into the closet."[7]

So how is it that LGBT people and young people can be treated differently? That's where the "art" of law comes in, and to understand *that*, you need to know some basics.

Some Basics about Law

First, as mentioned earlier, laws are *written* rules, and things written down are subject to interpretation.

More specifically, laws are written rules of *behavior*. There are laws about what everybody has to do (pay taxes), about what people shouldn't do (endanger others, such as by driving over the speed limit), and about what people must never do (deliberately harm others, such as through assaults or publishing falsehoods). The goal of these rules is to create an environment in which many people can live together in relative peace and safety.

Some people try to achieve this communal peace by trying to make everyone behave like them, but in the United States, when governments make laws, they must identify a good reason for establishing and enforcing laws—one that, at the very least, is rational.

Already we're into fuzzy territory, for what is "rational"? But setting that question aside for a minute, it's important to know that laws need a rational reason for existing. Many laws are created for the rational reason of protecting the health and safety of citizens, and some are created to protect young people in particular. For instance, forcing young children to work in factories may be acceptable in some countries, but in the United States, we believe there are rational reasons to prohibit such practices.

While centuries ago laws were said to come from "God" through the head of a church or a kingdom, today, in American democracy, laws come from the people through four basic sources: the Constitution, the legislature, administrative agencies, and the courts. And the scope with which they apply are federal (national), state, and local.

Constitutional laws are contained in a constitution, and virtually every government has a constitution—whether federal, state, or local. A constitution is a document that explains how a government will be set up, how it will operate, and what its overall values will be. Laws within a constitution were either created when the government was first formed or added at a later date through a special process for amending the document.

In the United States, there is one federal constitution—known, aptly enough, as the Constitution of the United States, or the U.S. Constitution. There is also, for each of the fifty states, a "state constitution" governing that state. And, for most municipalities and towns, there is a local constitution, usually referred to as a "charter."

While state constitutions and local charters apply only to the people who live and work within the specific state or municipality for which they are written, they cannot deny you any right that is granted to you by the U.S. Constitution. They can, however, grant you *more* rights than the U.S. Constitution. That is why some states were able to legalize sex between same-sex partners even *after* the U.S. Supreme Court ruled in 1986 that the federal constitution did not protect a citizen's right to privacy in choosing a same-sex partner.

Statutory laws (or "statutes") are laws created by the government's legislative body to protect the people's interests in the ever-changing world. At the federal level, these laws are referred to collectively and formally as the United States Code, and less formally as "federal statutes" or "federal acts." At the state level, they are generally called "state laws" or codes. And at the local level, they are referred to as "local ordinances."

You can look up a federal statute fairly easily. Many public libraries carry the volumes of the U.S. Code, and you can find it on the World

Wide Web by typing in http://uscode.house.gov. The citation for a federal statute usually looks something like this: 20 U.S.C. 7133. That's shorthand for "Title 20 of the United States Code, Section 7133." State codes can be similarly accessed.[8]

Administrative laws are rules and regulations made by governmental departments or agencies (such as the U.S. Department of Education or a state housing agency) that explain how laws by the legislature are to be enforced.

Common laws are laws that have evolved over the centuries from court rulings, rather than having been created by legislative bodies or agencies.

The Body Eclectic

One way to understand the differences among these types of laws is to think of the Constitution as the human body. Statutes are like clothing. Administrative laws might be likened to accessories. And common laws are overcoats.

As with the human body, major changes to a constitution are seldom made. Amputations can be performed, and surgery can change the function of certain organs within the body, but these changes are generally done for significant reasons and require difficult procedures. To amend the U.S. Constitution, both Congress and all fifty state legislatures must be involved.

Statutes are less dramatic than amendments. Just as circumstances outside—such as weather and fashion trends—can influence what clothes you wear, so, too, can circumstances prompt the creation of new statutes or changes to existing ones. Statutes, like clothing, are relatively easy to create and change. Congress can create or change a federal statute all by itself. (While the president signs a statute into effect, Congress has the ability to enact a law even without the president's signature—if the president chooses to neither sign nor veto it.)

In the same way that what clothing you wear is generally influenced by what kind of body you have, statutes are generally influenced by the

Constitution. Constitutional laws dictate general values and principles, and statutes dictate specific boundaries. For instance, the U.S. Constitution gave Congress the power to establish an army and a navy; and the Congress passed a statute in 1993 that very narrowly limited the circumstances under which an LGBT person would be allowed to serve in the military.[9]

Just as statutes relate to the Constitution, administrative laws relate to statutes. They are like wristwatches, belts, and hats, because they can vary greatly depending on what statutes are in effect—just as accessories tend to vary with what clothing you choose to wear.

Administrative laws are created by departments and agencies of experts in particular areas. For instance, at the U.S. Department of Health and Human Services, there are many doctors, medical researchers, social workers, and others with expertise in dealing with health issues, such as HIV infection, and people with social service needs, such as people without homes. These experts create regulations to carry out the mandates contained in statutes passed by the legislatures. Sometimes these mandates are fairly general—as in protecting the public health. For instance, the U.S. Congress created the Department of Health and Human Services to serve as the government's principle agency for protecting the health of all Americans and providing essential human services—such as shelter—for those who cannot obtain them for themselves. When the HIV virus first began spreading in the early 1980s, the U.S. Department of Health and Human Services created rules governing blood donations, including rules barring men who had sex with men from donating to blood banks.

At the local level, a local school board often creates the administrative laws concerning certain matters in the schools. For instance, school boards decide under what circumstances certain clubs—such as gay-straight alliances—can meet on school property, or how school administrators and teachers should respond when they hear a report of one student harassing another for being gay.

Common laws are rules that come into being when a judge or a court rules on a dispute, and they tend to be based on prior rulings. For example, says family law expert Roberta L. Murawski, "family statutes throughout the country say that judges need to make custody decisions 'in the best interests of the children.' "[10]

Meaning in the Mundane

The most influential constitution in the United States is the U.S. Constitution, because it governs the entire country. State constitutions govern only the state. As mentioned above, state constitutions must protect the same rights that are protected in the U.S. Constitution but they can promise *more*. They can also limit rights that the U.S. Constitution doesn't talk about. For instance, twenty-seven states in recent years have passed amendments to their constitutions to limit the legal definition of marriage in those states to that between one man and one woman;[11] the U.S. Constitution does not, at the time of this book's publication, define or limit marriage.[12]

Generally speaking, the same relationship exists between state constitutions and local charters.[13]

As mentioned earlier, constitutions typically do two things: organize government, and set forth basic values for their people. Both aspects can affect you as an LGBT person.

In laying out how the U.S. government is to be organized, the U.S. Constitution explains that it is to have three branches—the legislative (a Congress with a Senate and a House of Representatives), executive (a president), and judicial (federal courts). It also explains how and when the government's leaders will be elected and what the process is for creating laws.

The U.S. Constitution also explains how the federal government and the various state governments will interact. A good example is Article IV, Section 1, which states:

> Full faith and credit shall be given in each state to the public acts, records, and judicial proceedings of every other state. And the Con-

gress may by general laws prescribe the manner in which such acts, records, and proceedings shall be proved, and the effect thereof.

Often you'll hear this referred to as the "full faith and credit clause," which may not sound like something that has particular relevance to LGBT people, but it may ultimately determine whether a marriage license obtained by a same-sex couple in one state, such as Massachusetts, will be honored in another state.

When the Constitution was written, the full faith and credit clause was added to provide some sense of unity among the states even though each could make its own laws regarding a wide variety of matters. For instance, each state can make its own laws regarding the age at which a person can obtain a driver's license.

If states did not give full faith and credit to the laws of other states, then a fourteen-year-old who holds a driver's license in Arkansas would not be able to drive anywhere outside his or her home state, where the minimum age for driving is fifteen. A sixteen-year-old in New York would not be able to drive into New Jersey, where the driving-age minimum is seventeen.

If states did not give full faith and credit to the laws of other states, then an eighteen-year-old man and woman married in Texas would not be considered married in Mississippi, which requires prospective spouses to be at least twenty-one to marry.

But states *do* respect the laws of other states. The degree to which the U.S. Constitution's clause about full faith and credit requires states to respect each other's marriage laws is almost certainly to be tested in the next few years around same-sex marriage. The key argument against recognizing same-sex marriages from other states will likely be one based on the notion that one state can disregard another state's law if the other state's law conflicts with the first state's public policy.[14] It will almost certainly be argued that states that have passed constitutional amendments and statutes to prohibit recognition of same-sex marriages in their own states have a public policy against same-sex marriage. In those cases, the U.S. Supreme Court will have to rule whether such policies allow them to refuse to recognize a same-sex marriage licensed by another state, for example Massachusetts, while recognizing a heterosexual marriage licensed by that same state.[15] What complicates the answer to that question is that the U.S. Constitution also requires "equal protection"—that is, when people are in similar circumstances, the law must treat them equally.

In explaining how government is set up, constitutions also explain how laws are made. The U.S. Constitution explains that the United States' laws are made by Congress. State constitutions explain that state laws are made by state legislatures or general assemblies. For localities, laws can be made by a city council, a board of selectmen, or some other body of representatives elected by the people.

In some states, laws can also be made by a vote of the citizens at the ballot box (in a referendum or ballot initiative). Many antigay laws have been adopted this way, including laws to ban same-sex marriage. But even laws passed by a majority of the citizens are subject to scrutiny by the courts to determine whether they violate the constitution. As we saw in Chapter 3, in November 1992 voters in Colorado passed a measure, Amendment 2, to amend the state constitution to say that no one with a "homosexual, lesbian, or bisexual orientation" could seek redress for discrimination based on their sexual orientation. If you lived in Colorado and this law had gone into effect, a hotel could have refused to rent you a room because you're gay and you would have had no legal recourse. A landlord could have put up a sign that said, "Apartment for Rent; No Lesbians Need Apply."

The Colorado initiative, though passed by a majority of voters, was struck down by the U.S. Supreme Court in *Romer v. Evans* in 1996 as a violation of the U.S. Constitution's guarantee of equal protection.

A constitution also explains the circumstances under which it can be changed. Again, while Congress can pass statutes by simple majority votes in both the Senate and House of Representatives, an amendment to the U.S. Constitution requires the approval of two-thirds of each chamber of Congress and three-fourths of all state legislatures.

The second thing constitutions typically do—and the thing that most Americans know about the U.S. Constitution—is set out the government's basic values and principles and its guarantee of certain rights to its citizenry. The Preamble to the U.S. Constitution explains that one of the Constitution's purposes is to "secure the blessings of liberty to ourselves and our posterity." Various amendments to the Constitution guarantee that each citizen will have "equal protection of the law," and various freedoms—such as the freedom of press, speech, and religion, and that laws will be clear and applied fairly.

These important values and principles are considered to be vital aspects of the nation's character. To remove or change such core values would amount to a radical political upheaval. It is highly unlikely, for instance, that a majority of Americans would agree to a constitutional amendment that would limit the equal-protection guarantee. For that reason, opponents of equal protection for LGBT people and other minorities try to couch their proposals in other terms. For instance, a proposed constitutional amendment to ban legal recognition of same-sex marriage would give LGBT people *less protection* under the law as compared with heterosexuals. But proponents of such a ban veer away from this type of language; they claim to seek only to limit the definition of marriage to that between one man and one woman. If you're not paying close attention, *limiting the definition* doesn't sound so bad; to use our clothes metaphor, it's like making a fashion statement. But if you listen carefully, you see that what they really want to do is chop off the Constitution's equal-protection limb.

One additional important note about the Constitution: It protects the people from the *government*. It promises that the government—the legislature, the health department, the public schools, and other public agencies and officials—will not censor the people's speech or infringe upon their religions or take away their rights.

"For any protection against a *private* party (e.g., a private employer, private business, private school)," writes constitutional law expert Chai Feldblum, the people "have to depend on statutory rights."[16]

Dressing the Constitution

A statute can make it *look* like a limb's been cut off. For example, many states have sought to ban same-sex marriage by passing changes to their marriage statutes in order to dictate that licenses can't be issued to same-sex couples. The effect is the same when you go to a local courthouse to get a marriage license with your same-sex partner: the town or city clerk, bound by a state law, refuses to issue one. But when the ban is the product of a *statute,* you can sue, arguing that the state constitution's requirement for equal protection trumps the statute. (You can also sue based on your *constitutional* rights if a clerk, even absent a statute, refuses to issue you a license.)

Laws created by Congress are federal statutes and apply throughout the United States. Laws created by state legislatures are state laws and apply only in the state where a legislature has passed them. And of course, laws created by local governing bodies apply only in the city or town that has adopted them.

Statutory laws can deal with a wide range of subject matters, such as at what age a young man must register for the military, what criteria a couple must meet to obtain a marriage license, and what permits are necessary in order to stage a demonstration on a town's Main Street.

Federal statutes must abide by the federal constitution; state statutes must abide by both the federal and state constitutions; and local ordinances must be in accordance with the federal and state constitutions as well as the local governing charter. And this is where the "art" of law begins. As mentioned earlier, a judge compares the law and the constitution and renders his or her interpretation of whether the statute runs afoul of the constitution.

Because this is an *interpretation,* judges don't always agree. If there is a disagreement about whether a statute violates the federal constitution, the U.S. Constitution dictates that the federal courts will settle those disputes. When the lower federal courts disagree, it is up to the U.S. Supreme Court to decide the constitutionality of the statute.

Imagine that your high school principal says you can't wear your "trans pride" T-shirt to school and you sue, arguing that the prohibition violates your right to freedom of speech under the U.S. Constitution. Let's say another student in another state has the same experience and also files a lawsuit. The federal court where you live rules in your favor, stating that your T-shirt message is a legitimate exercise of freedom of expression and poses no danger to anyone. The federal court in the state where the other student lives says that that student's T-shirt message may be an exercise of freedom of expression but that the principal at the student's high school had good reason to believe that the T-shirt would provoke a violent reaction from other students. The cases could end right there: you go to school wearing your T-shirt and the other student wears something else to school. Or the losing side in each case could appeal the decision to the next highest level.

Federal courts and most state court systems have three levels—the entry level, usually known as a "district court," and two levels of appeals courts, an intermediate court, or court of appeal, and a high-level court, or supreme court.

Your lawsuit starts at the entry-level court. In the federal system, this is called the "U.S. District Court." (In a state court system, it's usually called the "state district court" or "county court" or "superior court.")

When this lowest level of court has ruled and the losing party of a lawsuit appeals, the appeal goes to the intermediate appeals court. In the federal system, this is known as the U.S. Court of Appeals. (In state courts, it is also typically known as the "state court of appeal" or "courts of appeal.") There are fewer of these and they are each designated to hear appeals from a specific region, known as a circuit. The "U.S. Court of Appeals for the First Circuit," for example, handles appeals from four states in the northeast region of the United States plus Puerto Rico.

In the federal court system, an appeal is first heard by a panel of three judges from the circuit court. If the losing party doesn't like the ruling, it can ask for review by the "full court" (also referred to by the French phrase "en banc"—pronounced "on bonk"). Once the full circuit court has weighed in on a lawsuit, there is only one appeals court left—the U.S. Supreme Court. (At the state level, this is typically called the state supreme court.) Between seven thousand and eight thousand cases per year are appealed to the U.S. Supreme Court but only about one hundred are actually argued and only about eighty to ninety of those result in a written decision.

Most appeals to the U.S. Supreme Court are simply turned away—the appeals (called petitions) are "denied." When that happens, the circuit court's opinion remains intact but its opinion applies only in those states that comprise the circuit. (Similarly, if a circuit court refuses to hear an appeal, the district court's opinion remains intact but applies only in that district court's jurisdiction.)

Disputes over whether state laws violate the state constitution are settled in state courts and may ultimately be decided by a state's supreme court. Questions about the legal validity of local ordinances are also decided in state courts.

Like citizens, different judges can disagree on whether a statute violates a constitution. That's because the job of courts is to interpret the language of the constitution, and in some cases that involves interpreting the meaning of such terms as "liberty" and "privacy." It's not easy. Ask yourself: Does "liberty" mean solely the ability to move about freely or does it mean the right to make certain decisions for yourself? Does the right to privacy mean that you can do anything you want in the privacy of your own home? And while the word "liberty" does appear in the U.S. Constitution, the word "privacy" does not. Does that mean that the Constitution shouldn't protect a right to privacy?

Judging statutes against the language of constitutions is a tricky business. It can be quite subjective and, therefore, vulnerable to the political and personal prejudices of judges and the people. A good example of this can be seen in the different interpretations of statutes banning same-sex sexual relations in 1986 and 2003.

The question before the U.S. Supreme Court in two landmark cases looked at the constitutionality of laws in certain states prohibiting sexual relations between two consenting adults in the privacy of their home. The Constitution says nothing *explicitly* about sexual relations between any two adults, but, as explained in Chapter 4, the U.S. Supreme Court has interpreted certain language in the Constitution as *implicitly* protecting a right to privacy when it comes to intimate relations between adults.

When it came to determining whether there was also a right to privacy covering intimate relations in same-sex sexual relationships, the U.S. Supreme Court first ruled, in 1986, that there *wasn't;* but seventeen years later it ruled that there *was.*

In the first case, *Bowers v. Hardwick,* the Supreme Court noted that, while its previous rulings acknowledged that the Constitution protects an *implicit right* to privacy for married heterosexual couples in matters of family, marriage, and procreation, sexual activity between two same-sex adults did not bear "any resemblance" to these matters.

In the second case, *Lawrence v. Texas* in 2003, the Supreme Court ruled that the U.S. Constitution's *explicit guarantee* of "liberty" does protect the right of adults to engage in sex with a partner of the same sex.

In each case, the Court was asked to rule on a different provision—explicit or implicit—of the Constitution, and in each case, it reached a different conclusion. Although some Court observers argue that the different result was due to the political leanings of the justices on the Supreme Court at the time of the decisions, there is no denying that the Court's mandate, nevertheless, is to make its decisions based on its best and fairest interpretation of the Constitution.

There is also no denying that the impact of each of those decisions on the lives of sexual minorities was enormous.

After the *Hardwick* decision upheld so-called sodomy statutes in 1986, numerous negative actions against sexual minorities were taken, citing *Hardwick* as their justification.

Upcoming legal battles around marriage statutes, freedom-of-expression issues, and many other matters important to LGBT people will likely be scrutinized in the coming years—from the rights to privacy and liberty, to equal protection, and even the more obscure full faith and credit provision. Who the justices are and how they interpret the law in those cases will almost certainly have a direct impact on your life as an LGBT person.

7

Sex
Legal and Not

Sooner or later, you're going to have sex—unless, of course, you're among the 10 percent of men and 8 percent of women who've never had sex at all.[1] If you *are* going to have sex, there's good news and bad news, legally speaking.

The good news is that same-sex sexual activity is no longer illegal anywhere in the United States. The bad news is that there are still ways in which your sexual activity with a partner of the same sex could get you into legal trouble. In fact, it might be against the law for you to even *ask* someone to have sex with you.

The Good—No, the *Best* News

The history here bears repeating: Hard as it is to believe, sex between consenting adults of the same gender was a crime in *every* state up until 1961, and a felony in some. In 1986, when the U.S. Supreme Court upheld the constitutionality of laws prohibiting same-sex sexual relations, twenty-four states and the District of Columbia still outlawed such sex. By 2003, only thirteen of those states still had so-called sodomy laws, because laws in the others had been invalidated by state supreme court decisions.

But on June 26, 2003—a date that merits a celebration in the history of LGBT people along with the Stonewall Rebellion of June 27, 1969—the U.S. Supreme Court issued a new opinion concerning sodomy laws. This time, it said that such laws were unconstitutional—that they violated the right to liberty and due process.

The 2003 ruling in *Lawrence v. Texas* is probably not one you're going to be taught in high school, but as an LGBT person, it is one that has a tremendous amount of influence on your life; it is one that could, potentially, be overturned, and so it's definitely worth taking the time to learn about.

First of all, you might be wondering how a case such as this—or its predecessor, *Bowers v. Hardwick*—ever got into court in the first place. After all, if people are having sex *in the privacy of their own homes*, how could they be arrested, right?

In both cases, the gay men who challenged the law were having sex in the privacy of their own bedrooms. In Hardwick's case, a police officer in Atlanta went to Hardwick's apartment to arrest him for allegedly failing to pay a fine on a misdemeanor (even though he had, in fact, paid the fine). A friend of Hardwick's was asleep on the couch in the living room and answered the door when the officer arrived and allowed him to enter the apartment. The officer found Hardwick in his bedroom, engaged in sex with another man. The officer arrested both men for violating the state's sodomy law; only Hardwick challenged the law, but he was unsuccessful in his attempt.

John Lawrence and Tyron Garner were having sex in the privacy of their own bedroom when a neighbor in Houston called police to claim that someone with a gun had entered their home and was firing shots. The report was a false one, apparently intended to harass the men, but police entered the home and found the two men engaged in sex. They, too, challenged the law, but their lawsuit, pressed by Lambda Legal Defense and Education Fund, was successful, leading to an enormous improvement in the legal and political landscape for LGBT people.

With sodomy statutes struck down, the laws could no longer be used to arrest people for having sexual partners of the same sex. They could also no longer be used against LGBT people in many other contexts—to justify firing them from jobs, affect their ability to hold public office, limit their child custody and visitation rights, prohibit sexual-minority groups from receiving public funding, and even justify censorship of homosexual content on public television programs.[2] More generally, it meant that people who had sex with partners of the same sex could no longer be viewed as outlaws.

On its most basic level, the Supreme Court decision in *Lawrence* said simply that the government may not prohibit consensual sex in a private setting between people of the same sex. Legally speaking, it said two more things that are of importance to LGBT people:

1. The "liberty" protected by the Fourteenth Amendment includes the right of "homosexual persons" to choose with whom to engage in "certain intimate conduct," including sex.
2. Government may not prohibit sex between same-sex couples, because the Fourteenth Amendment to the Constitution holds that a state may not "deprive any person of life, liberty, or property, without due process of law."

"Due process of law" is a legal term that defines certain ground rules for laws—laws must, as we discussed earlier, be established for some definable good reason, and they must be applied fairly. You will sometimes hear lawyers talk about "substantive due process" and "procedural due process." Substantive refers to the reasons for the law; procedural refers to how fairly the laws are enforced. And this is where the bad news comes in.

The Bad News

Believe it or not, less than a year *after* the Supreme Court struck down all state laws prohibiting same-sex sexual relations, a state appeals court in Kansas upheld the conviction of an eighteen-year-old male for having sex with another teenage male.[3] A man in Virginia was convicted for *asking* another man to have sex with him.[4] He spent eight days in jail. And if you live in a group home, such as with a foster care family or a residence for youth in need of shelter, sex with another resident is still illegal regardless of whether that person is of the same or other sex.

How could that be? After all, we've just discussed how the U.S. Supreme Court, in 2003's *Lawrence v. Texas* decision, struck down laws prohibiting same-sex sexual relations. Well, in the first two instances, lawsuits are asking the courts to define just how far the *Lawrence* ruling extends. In the third instance, there are simply some places and some conditions under which sexual activity is prohibited whether the partners are the same sex or not. For instance, it is illegal to have sex:

- in public;
- in exchange for money;
- when one of the parties does not consent;[5]
- when one of the parties is underage.

In some states, it is illegal to have sex with someone to whom you are not married; in some states, it is illegal to have sex with someone who is married to someone else.[6]

These examples probably raise some big questions for you. For instance, you might be wondering whether "public" includes the backseat of a car. How about the lavatory in an airplane? Does a sexual partner have to make a statement of willingness to have sex in order for there to be "consent"? What's "underage"? What if both partners are underage?

The answers to these questions are determined by *state* laws and they vary from state to state. For instance, in the state of New York, it would be illegal for you to have sex in your own bedroom if it could be "easily visible from or in any public street, sidewalk or thoroughfare."[7] In Illinois, it's a crime for an unmarried person to have sexual intercourse "with another not his spouse" if the unmarried person "knows that the other person involved in such intercourse is married."[8] And in almost every state, prostitution is prohibited. But in Nevada, only anal and oral sex are prohibited in public, prostitution is unlawful "except in a licensed house of prostitution," and adultery is not a crime.[9]

It's especially important to know your state's laws concerning age of consent. Some state laws are fairly simple; they state an age at which a young person is considered capable of giving consent to have sex. Some are more complicated. For instance, in Alaska, you can have sex as young as sixteen but your sexual partner cannot be under thirteen years of age. It's also illegal in Alaska for a sixteen-year-old to "aid, induce, cause, or encourage" someone under the age of thirteen to have sex. And if you're eighteen in Alaska, your sexual partner cannot be younger than sixteen.[10]

So if you want to know the answer to any of these questions specific to where you live, you'll want to check your state's laws. This is something you can do at most public libraries by asking the reference desk for the "state code." (Just as all federal statutes are referred to as the "U.S. Code," so state laws in most states are referred to simply as "The California Code," "The Code of Massachusetts," or the "North Carolina General Statutes.") On the Web, an easy way to find your state code is to go to the FindLaw Web site, click on "Cases & Codes," and then click on "U.S. State Laws." Once you click on your state's code, you'll often get a list of "Titles."

Get a Room!

In addition to knowing what the law is, you may want to think about law enforcement. For instance, there are laws in most states against having sex in public, but whenever a straight couple gets really physical in full view of others, the reaction from law enforcement is likely to be along the lines of "Get a room!" To some extent, society tolerates public displays of affection between heterosexual partners, and to some extent police officers have leeway in deciding when to enforce the law. But if a same-sex couple should "get frisky" in public, neither society nor police tend to be lenient.

"Having sex where others might see you and take offense can subject you to arrest, publicity and other serious consequences," according to Lambda.[11] Before you even consider having sex in public, you should consider the potential consequences. In fact, there are things you need to think about before you even consider talking in public with someone about having sex.

In March 2003—three months before the U.S. Supreme Court struck down state sodomy laws—Joel Singson was in a public restroom in Virginia Beach, Virginia, when he suggested to a man who was also in the restroom that they have sex. The other man turned out to be an undercover police officer, who arrested Singson for solicitation to commit a crime. Remember, at the time, sodomy was still illegal in Virginia and twelve other states. By the time the case went to trial, however, the sodomy law had been struck down, so Lambda argued that Singson could no longer be guilty of soliciting to commit a crime. However, the police officer claimed that Singson invited him to have sex *in the public restroom*—a claim that Singson denies—and the trial court believed the police officer. So the solicitation charge was treated as a solicitation to have sex in public, which is illegal.[12]

Lambda recommends that you exercise a great deal of caution when discussing a possible sexual encounter with a same-sex person you don't know. Among other things, it recommends the following:

- *Always carry identification.* Should you be arrested, having proper identification could help reduce the likelihood you'd spend time in jail.
- *Tell a friend where you are.* If you're meeting someone whom you've been corresponding with on the Internet, tell someone—or leave a note—saying where you're going, who you're meeting, and when you expect to return.
- *Know what to do if you're arrested.* Provide police with your identification but don't answer any other questions until you've obtained a lawyer. (If you can't afford one, ask that a public defender be appointed to you.) Notice as many details as possible—place, time, and circumstances leading up to arrest; officers' names and badge numbers; and whether any witnesses might have been present.
- *Stay away from minors.* Unless you are a minor, having sex with or soliciting sex from a person who is under the age of consent is illegal.

The Age of Consent

Which brings us to another important law that varies from state to state—age of consent. As discussed earlier, in order to protect minors from adults who might sexually abuse or exploit them, states define an "age of consent." These laws stipulate at what age a person is old enough —legally speaking—to be able to decide whether to have sex. (These differ from "age of majority" laws that define at what age a person is old enough to be treated as an adult for other legal purposes, such as signing contracts.) Until you reach the age of consent defined by your state's law, you can't *legally* have sex, not even if your parents say it's OK. The law says it's not OK for you to have sex until you're old enough to voluntarily consent—and the law decides when you're "old enough."

This *also* applies to the age of the person with whom you choose to have sex. If you're old enough but your partner is not, you may be committing a crime (statutory rape), even if that person consents to having sex with you.

The key pieces of information you need, as a young person, are:

• what the age of consent is in your state;
• how old your sexual partner is.

Age of consent varies from state to state. In Virginia, the age of consent is fifteen. In California, it's eighteen. In Iowa, it's fourteen.[13] Many Web sites purport to provide age-of-consent information for each of the states, but many are outdated or inaccurate in other ways. If you have trouble finding the information through your state's code, the U.S. Department of Justice's National Criminal Justice Reference Center recommends the Web site promotetruth.org, which provides references to each state's code.[14]

But the law gets even more complicated than with respect to age alone. If both sexual partners are under eighteen, the law also puts some limits on how many years difference in age there can be between them. For instance, look at the law in North Carolina:

§ 14-27.7A. Statutory rape or sexual offense of person who is 13, 14, or 15 years old.

(a) A defendant is guilty of a Class B1 felony if the defendant engages in vaginal intercourse or a sexual act with another person who is 13, 14, or 15 years old and the defendant is at least six years older than the person, except when the defendant is lawfully married to the person.

(b) A defendant is guilty of a Class C felony if the defendant engages in vaginal intercourse or a sexual act with another person who is 13, 14, or 15 years old and the defendant is more than four but less than six years older than the person, except when the defendant is lawfully married to the person.

Confused? It gets even *more* complicated. North Carolina also has this law:

§ 14-202.1. Taking indecent liberties with children.

(a) A person is guilty of taking indecent liberties with children if, being 16 years of age or more and at least five years older than the child in question, he either:

   (1) Willfully takes or attempts to take any immoral, improper, or indecent liberties with any child of either sex under the age of 16 years for the purpose of arousing or gratifying sexual desire; or

   (2) Willfully commits or attempts to commit any lewd or lascivious act upon or with the body or any part or member of the body of any child of either sex under the age of 16 years.

(b) Taking indecent liberties with children is punishable as a Class F felony.

Being the older partner in a sexual act with a person who is not legally deemed to be able to consent could land you in jail for statutory rape.[15] In Missouri, where the age of consent is fourteen, it is still considered statutory rape if a person who is twenty-one has sex with a person who is sixteen.[16] As you can see, it's very different and even some-what unpredictable state to state. To be safe, you really need to read your state's law and make sure that both you and your sexual partner are legally of age to have sex with each other.

This aspect of the law is one that, like that concerning sex in public, has been enforced more stringently against LGBT people than against heterosexuals. A good case in point is what happened to Matthew Limon in Kansas. Limon had just turned eighteen when he had sex with a male teenager at a residential school for young people with developmental disabilities. The other teen was fourteen, and the Kansas age of consent is fourteen.[17] However, like North Carolina, Kansas has a law against "indecent liberties with a child" for instances in which an adult has sex with a minor who is fourteen or fifteen years old.[18] Kansas law prohibits sex between partners if one person is between fourteen and sixteen years of age and the other is "less than nineteen years of age and less than four years of age older" than the other person, but it makes the penalty much harsher if the partners are of the same sex.[19]

Had Matthew's partner been a female, notes the American Civil Liberties Union, which pressed a lawsuit on his behalf, he would have been sentenced to no more than fifteen months for the same offense.

But in Matthew's case, because his partner was of the same sex, Matthew was convicted—in February 2000—of violating the state's law against sodomy and sentenced to more than seventeen years in prison.[20]

One last note: When looking up your state's age-of-consent laws, be sure that you're looking at age of consent for *sexual activity*; in some states, the age of consent for *marriage* is different.

8

Pleading the First

Chances are, when you learned about the First Amendment in high school, you never thought, "Oh, that could affect what I wear to school one day." You probably didn't consider that it might have some impact on your ability to kiss your girlfriend or boyfriend in school. And you certainly didn't think, "Hey, that could determine whether or not my picture's in the yearbook."

Think again. The First Amendment is a pervasive and powerful thing.

It's just forty-five words long. But if you're part of a sexual minority—or any minority—it's forty-five words worth memorizing, because the constitutional issues that come up most frequently for sexual-minority youth are all contained in this one sentence:

> Congress shall make no law respecting an establishment of religion, or prohibiting the free exercise thereof; or abridging the freedom of speech, or of the press; or the right of the people peaceably to assemble, and to petition the Government for a redress of grievances.

So, you're probably already wondering, "Where's the part that says I can kiss my girlfriend or boyfriend in school?"

It's Not Just What You Say

Consider the case of a high school student in Orange County, California, in 2005. Charlene Nguon was a bright student. Out of 421 other juniors at her high school, she ranked twentieth academically. She was active in several school clubs, and teachers were very complimentary about her "good attitude" and "hard work." She was also a lesbian who was not afraid to hug and kiss her girlfriend at school.

As you probably know, straight students in high school can be affectionate with their girlfriends and boyfriends and that's not usually viewed as a problem. But Charlene's displays of affection to her girlfriend were a problem in the eyes of her principal, Ben Wolf. According to the lawsuit filed by the American Civil Liberties Union, Wolf "repeatedly punished" Charlene—including with suspensions—"because she dared to be openly lesbian" at school. A school counselor called Charlene into her office and ordered her to stop displaying affection toward her girlfriend. And the principal called her mother to complain that Charlene was kissing another girl—without first asking Charlene whether she was out to her mother.

Imagine your parents getting *that* phone call. Fortunately for Charlene, her mother agreed to help her fight back. Because Charlene had not yet reached the age of majority in California, her mother filed a lawsuit on her behalf.

When you're under the age of majority in your state, you can't file a lawsuit in your own name. Legally, you need a "next friend" to file it in their name. "Next friend" is a legal term that indicates that the party to the lawsuit—in this case, Charlene—is not old enough to file the lawsuit herself, so an adult has done so on her behalf. If your parent is unwilling or unable to file as your "next friend," some other legally competent person, such as another relative, can do so.[1] Or the court can appoint a "guardian ad litem" to serve in the role.

Charlene's lawsuit, *Nguon v. Wolf*, filed by the ACLU, charged the school with violating Charlene's First Amendment right to free speech. School officials weren't trying to prevent Charlene from *saying* anything, but they tried to stop her from doing things that expressed things about herself that they didn't want to see. Legally speaking, these acts, on her part, amounted to "expressive conduct."

And, as the lawsuit noted, school officials "disciplined Nguon for expressive conduct that is not similarly punished when engaged in by students who are not gay, lesbian, or bisexual."

Charlene's lawsuit is a great example of how many laws—constitutional and statutory, state and federal—can be called into action to protect young people's right to decide for themselves who they are and how and when they will share that information with others. In addition to violating her First Amendment right to freedom of speech, the lawsuit charged school officials with violating:

- the U.S. Constitution's guarantee of equal protection when they tried to stop Charlene from displaying affection to her girlfriend but did nothing to stop straight students exhibiting the same behaviors with their partners;
- the U.S. Constitution's guarantee of a right to privacy when the principal, without Charlene's permission, revealed to Charlene's mother that her daughter was gay;
- the California Constitution's guarantees of free speech, equal protection, and privacy;
- a California education law that prohibits discrimination based on sexual orientation;
- the state's Unruh Civil Rights Act (which does not explicitly prohibit sexual-orientation discrimination but which has been interpreted by California courts as doing so implicitly).

Charlene's case is also a good illustration of how quickly a lawsuit can remedy an injustice but how long it might take for that lawsuit to work. Charlene's problems with school officials began in December 2004, when she was in her junior year. The lawsuit was filed in September 2005, as she was entering her senior year. Attorneys representing the school officials asked the court—the U.S. District Court for the Central District of California—to dismiss the case. (For a number of reasons, that's a pretty routine move on the part of attorneys defending a client, for a number of reasons—one of which is to delay progression of the lawsuit in hopes of wearing down the plaintiff's resolve, running up the expenses the plaintiff will have to pay an attorney,[2] or rendering the issue moot.[3]) A federal judge ruled on the request to dismiss in November 2005. (He refused to dismiss it.) The case had just gone to trial in December 2006. Charlene was in college, and a decision would likely be rendered in 2007.

In defending their actions concerning the privacy charge, school officials claimed that they had not violated her privacy, because she had been openly gay at school. A "reasonable person could not expect that their actions on school grounds, in front of everyone else on school grounds, would remain private." But in refusing to dismiss the case, the judge ruled that the disclosure to Charlene's mother was a "serious invasion of her privacy" and that just because her actions on school grounds were not wholly private did not mean that she had no interest in limiting disclosure or dissemination of information.

In a statement released by the ACLU, Charlene's mother expressed her satisfaction with the judge's ruling and its impact on other students.

"I love and fully support Charlene, but that's not the case for every gay student out there," said Nguon's mother, Crystal Chhun. "The person to decide when and how to talk with our family about her sexual orientation should have been my daughter, not the principal."[4]

It *Can* Be What You Say

So, one form of "speech" is behavior. That's why you'll sometimes hear "freedom of speech" spoken of as freedom of *expression*—because "expression" better conveys the scope of what the term covers.

And whether it's behavior or the written word or a spoken one, the freedom of speech protects your right to express your opinion. It protects your right to say that laws banning same-sex marriage are un-American. It protects the other guy—the guy who goes around school calling almost everybody he meets a "faggot"—to express his belief that he has an uncanny ability to identify gay people with just a glance and that we are, indeed, everywhere. And it protects the right of the girl next to you to say she believes homosexuality is a sin.

But what if somebody says something that's more troubling? What if they say, "Homosexuality is a sin, faggot, so I have to kill you!"

Threatening to kill someone is a crime, and most people know that. Now imagine someone corners you at school and says, in a menacing tone, "I'm going to get you after school, faggot." How do you know when a threat has crossed the line and become illegal?

The U.S. Supreme Court explains the answer as a matter of "proximity and degree":

> The question in every case is whether the words used are used in such circumstances and are of such a nature as to create a clear and present danger that they will bring about the substantive evils that Congress has a right to prevent.[5]

So what do you think? Is there a "clear and present danger" when a popular rap artist blares over your car radio, stating that his words are "like a dagger" stabbing gay people in the head? Probably not. For one thing, his image is a simile (*"like* a dagger"), and it is delivered as part of the lyrics to a rap song. The performer is not "present," but more likely thousands of miles away.

But what if the lyrics advise listeners to get a piece of rope and hang a lesbian with it? And what if the lyrics are being sung in a public park in a city with a large gay population?

LGBT people in some parts of the world have been able to stop public appearances by performers whose lyrics promote violence against sexual minorities. In London, an LGBT group called Outrage! complained about a reggae artist whose lyrics called for getting a gun and killing the "battyman" [Jamaican slang for gay man]. After police investigated the concerns and talked to officials of the nightclub where the artist was to appear, the nightclub canceled the singer's appearance due to concerns about public safety.

Concerts were also canceled for similar reasons in San Francisco and Los Angeles. And the Associated Press reported in July 2006 that a reggae concert in New York City to raise money to fight AIDS had been canceled because of concerns for public safety.[6] The concert was scheduled for a nightclub in the East Village.

But what if the message being delivered is one of LGBT pride? Can limitations be imposed on that? After all, it's not a message creating a clear and present danger to others. The surprise answer is "maybe."

First, take the case of Brad Mathewson, who in 2004 was a sixteen-year-old junior at Webb City High School in Webb City, Missouri. He wore a T-shirt to school one day that said "Gay/Straight Alliance" on the front and had a pink triangle and "Make a Difference" on the back. His homeroom teacher sent him to the assistant principal's office, telling him she thought the T-shirt was inappropriate. The assistant principal agreed, saying it was distracting and offensive to others.

Brad asked the assistant principal to explain why it was distracting and offensive, but the assistant principal would not explain. So Brad pointed out that other students at the school displayed stickers, note-books, and signs declaring that same-sex marriage is wrong. If they could express their view, certainly he should be able to express his more positive view about being gay. The assistant principal was still unmoved and told Brad he had to either go home and change or turn his pride T-shirt inside out so that no one could see the message.

So Brad headed to the school's bathroom to turn his shirt inside out. Along the way, he bumped into a straight friend and told him what had happened. They decided to exchange shirts. The straight student wore the "Gay/Straight Alliance" shirt openly all day and, surprisingly, no teacher or administrator asked him to remove it.

The following week, Brad decided to wear a T-shirt with the message, "I'm gay and I'm proud." One of his male friends wore a T-shirt saying, "I love lesbians." This time, the assistant principal demanded that both students change or turn the shirts inside out.

But this time, Brad refused and was forced to leave school. He called his mother, who came to school the following day to talk with school officials. School officials told her that the shirt was distracting, that it amounted to "flaunting" being gay, and that it could make Brad vulnerable to hostilities from other students. In other words, they were claiming that it posed a danger.

Brad's mother retained a lawyer to talk to school officials. The officials told the lawyer that Brad would not be allowed back at school unless he agreed not to wear T-shirts with progay messages. Meanwhile, that same day, Brad saw another student at school wearing a T-shirt with an *antigay* message.

With the help of the American Civil Liberties Union and his mother as "next friend," Brad filed a lawsuit in federal court, charging that the school officials' ban on progay messages on T-shirts violated his First Amendment right to free speech. He later dropped the lawsuit and dropped out of school, but his initial effort triggered some change. It inspired a straight friend and classmate, LaStaysha Myers, to challenge the policy.

First, with the help of her mother, she and some friends created their own T-shirts with messages of support for gay people, such as "I support gay rights." They wore the shirts to school and were stopped by school officials who told them the shirts were not allowed. LaStaysha and her friends refused the order to remove the shirts, and were sent home.

That night, LaStaysha and her mother created a new T-shirt: This one simply bore the definition of the word "gay" as copied out of a Webster's dictionary. She wore it to school the next day and, again, school officials told her she had to change the shirt. Again, LaStaysha refused and, again, school officials sent her home. All this time, LaStaysha and her mother noticed that students were allowed to wear T-shirts bearing antigay messages. So, with the help of the ACLU and her mother as "next friend," LaStaysha filed a lawsuit in federal court.[7]

"In part because she has gay relatives and friends, [LaStaysha] holds the political belief that gay people and their supporters should be treated with fairness and dignity," said the lawsuit. "Plaintiff also holds the political belief that gay people and their supporters should be able to express their progay political beliefs."

This time, the school relented and—even before the lawsuit went to trial—agreed to stop censoring students from wearing progay messages.

"All I ever wanted was to get my school to stop silencing me and allow all students to express their opinions, so I'm really happy that's finally going to happen," said LaStaysha, in an ACLU press release after the school made the agreement.[8]

So where does the "maybe" come in when we're talking about the right to express our views, regardless of how unpopular they may be with other students or school officials? The answer is a little like the example of shouting "Fire!" in a crowded theater. Consider the case of a student at a school where there had been frequent violent clashes between progay and antigay students.

In Poway, California, a sixteen-year-old student was suspended for wearing an antigay T-shirt that said "Be Ashamed, Our School has embraced what God has condemned. Homosexuality is shameful." It's an unpleasant message, to be sure, but not particularly threatening, right? Well, school officials were able to ban it. They noted, and a court agreed, that it was relevant that the school had been the site of numerous altercations between gays and nongays. That T-shirt was seen as both furthering that disruption and violating the Poway High School's dress code forbidding "violence or hate behavior, including derogatory connotations directed toward sexual identity."

Similar conflicts have arisen in other school districts over T-shirts, and new incidents continue to arise. But victories for freedom of expression are being won—often by gay and straight students working together. For instance, in Dublin, Ohio, in March 2005, the principal of the local high school made a student remove a T-shirt that read, "I support gay marriage." The next day, more students wore the T-shirt. The principal ordered them to change and even suspended one student who refused. The following day, even *more* students wore the T-shirts, bearing a message about the constitutional First Amendment right to freedom of expression.

Soon the ACLU of Ohio got involved, sending a letter to school officials and pointing out that the U.S. Supreme Court had ruled that students do not "shed their constitutional rights to freedom of speech or expression at the schoolhouse gate." The ACLU was referring to a U.S. Supreme Court ruling in February 1969 in connection with a famous lawsuit, *Tinker v. Des Moines.*[9] The lawsuit was filed by students who wanted to protest American involvement in the Vietnam War by wearing black armbands. The three student protesters were only thirteen, fourteen, and fifteen years old when they wore their black armbands to school. They were each sent home and told that school policy prohibited them from wearing armbands. As the Supreme Court ruling in their case noted:

> The school officials banned and sought to punish petitioners for a silent, passive expression of opinion, unaccompanied by any disorder or disturbance on the part of petitioners. There is here no evidence whatever of petitioners' interference, actual or nascent, with the schools' work or of collision with the rights of other students to be secure and to be let alone. . . .
>
> There is no indication that the work of the schools or any class was disrupted. Outside the classrooms, a few students made hostile remarks to the children wearing armbands, but there were no threats or acts of violence on school premises. . . .
>
> Any variation from the majority's opinion may inspire fear. Any word spoken, in class, in the lunchroom, or on the campus, that deviates from the views of another person may start an argument or cause a disturbance. But our Constitution says we must take this risk . . . ; and our history says that it is this sort of hazardous freedom—this kind of openness—that is . . . the basis of our national strength and of the independence and vigor of Americans who grow up and live in this relatively permissive, often disputatious, society.

Raising this decision in its letter to the superintendent of Dublin City Schools, the ACLU demanded that school officials stop barring students from wearing T-shirts with progay messages. This time, school officials agreed to stop censoring the T-shirts, again, even before a lawsuit was filed.

As the ACLU points out in its literature, the First Amendment "does not mean that you can put *anything* on your T-shirt and parade it around the campus."[10] The key is that the T-shirt cannot disrupt classes or infringe upon the rights of others to feel safe.

While school officials can't censor your shirt just because other students don't like the message, says the ACLU, they can censor it if they can show that that message amounts to "obscene, threatening, or 'lewd or vulgar' speech."[11]

The ACLU recommends that if a school official orders you not to wear a T-shirt with an LGBT pride message, "be polite and comply with any order from your principal or teacher," but take the following steps:

- Record the types of T-shirt messages that *are* allowed in your school.
- Take note of which school officials spoke to you, on what dates and at what times of day, and what they said.
- Keep a record of other students who were also ordered to change their shirts.
- Keep a copy of any written notice the school gives you concerning your shirt or school policy about T-shirt messages.
- Write down the names of anybody who witnessed the school official talking to you.
- Contact the ACLU at getequal@aclu.org or call (212) 549–2673. ("It's confidential—we won't ever contact your school, your parents, your friends, or anyone else without your okay, and any communication between you and the ACLU is private.")[12]

It Can Be Your Style of Clothes

Now, imagine for a moment that you're not the kind of person who is comfortable showing affection for your same-sex partner in front of others, and you're not really bold enough to wear a pride T-shirt at school. Maybe you've never even told anybody you're lesbian, gay, bisexual, or transgender. You might feel pretty confident that, because of these things, you're pretty safe from discrimination. Unless, of course, you wear clothes other people don't think you should wear.

Kevin Logan's high school principal in Gary, Indiana, banned him from attending his senior prom in May 2006 because he showed up in a formal dress and high heels. According to the Gender Public Advocacy Coalition (GenderPAC), the school claimed it was prohibiting his attendance in a dress because "student dress which causes an interference with his/her work or creates classroom or school disorder is by definition inappropriate." And yet school officials allowed a female student to attend wearing a tuxedo, and Kevin had worn dresses to school all year.[13]

Jennifer Harris, a member of the Pennsylvania State University women's basketball team, filed a lawsuit against that team's coach, Rene Portland, after Portland repeatedly badgered her to change her clothing, appearance, and demeanor so as to appear more "feminine."

Nikki Youngblood had worn "boys' clothing" since she was eight years old, including to school. But when she showed up wearing a suit jacket and tie to get her senior portrait taken for her Tampa, Florida, high school yearbook, school officials would not let her photo be taken. The only way the studio would take her picture, they said, was if she agreed to wear a very feminine-looking scoop-necked drape over her bare shoulders. Nikki refused to wear the drape and the school omitted her photo and even Nikki's name from the yearbook.

With the help of the National Center for Lesbian Rights (NCLR) and the Legal Advocacy Project of Equality Florida,[14] Nikki filed a lawsuit in federal court against the school in 2002, charging school officials with violating several constitutional and statutory laws, including:

- the First Amendment right to freedom of expression under the U.S. Constitution;
- the right to freedom of expression guaranteed in the Florida Constitution;
- the Fourteenth Amendment guarantee of equal protection under the U.S. Constitution;

• the "Basic Rights" guarantee of the Florida Constitution;
• Title IX of the federal Education Amendments of 1972, prohibiting sex discrimination;
• the Florida Educational Equity Act, prohibiting sex discrimination.

Laws prohibiting sex discrimination have sometimes rescued LGBT people from discrimination based on their sexual-minority status. As part of the federal Education Amendments of 1972, Congress passed a law—Title IX—to prohibit discrimination based on sex in any school or educational program that receives federal funding.[15] The law states that:

No person in the United States shall, on the basis of sex, be excluded from participation in, be denied the benefits of, or be subjected to discrimination under any education program or activity receiving Federal financial assistance.

At the district court level, Nikki lost. The lower court judge said, among other things, that the issue of what girls should wear for their senior portrait was too trivial a matter to be addressed by the court. He granted the school officials' request that the case be dismissed.

But NCLR and other groups—including the ACLU—appealed to the Eleventh Circuit U.S. Court of Appeals, which covers Florida, Georgia, and Alabama. In its brief to the Eleventh Circuit, the ACLU noted that the U.S. Supreme Court had, in a well-known case from 1989, ruled that "requiring individuals to conform to gender stereotypes, even when those stereotypes do not implicate immutable characteristics or infringe on fundamental rights, falls within the prohibitions in Title VII and the Equal Protection Clause on sex discrimination."[16]

Title VII is a section of the U.S. Civil Rights Act of 1964 that prohibits discrimination in employment based on race, color, religion, sex, and national origin, and has been interpreted by the U.S. Supreme Court to prohibit discrimination against a person for not adhering to sex stereotypes.[17]

Although Nikki's legal challenge wasn't about employment, noted the NCLR and others, "the Supreme Court has held that Title VII cases are relevant to the determination of what constitutes gender-based discrimination under Title IX."

At this point, school officials in Tampa relented and changed their policy of requiring girls to wear the feminine drape for their senior portraits.

"At first I was kind of discouraged by the whole thing," Nikki said in an interview with GenderPAC.[18] "But, then I realized that what they're doing is wrong. Maybe I can't get in my yearbook, but I can make it easier for the next person like me who comes along. At least she won't have to go through what I went through. If there's no one who has the courage to fight, this stuff never changes."

9

The Powers of Assembly

For decades after our nation ratified amendments to guarantee the rights of citizenship to African Americans, many people were still hostile to the idea of the law treating black people with the same respect it did whites. In the 1950s, that hostility played out in some states, primarily in the South, where state officials used the courts and law to prevent black people from meeting and organizing. Among other things, they would get court orders to intimidate such groups into turning over their membership lists to the state. When Alabama tried this tactic with the National Association for the Advancement of Colored People (NAACP), the group refused to comply and refused to pay a one-hundred-thousand-dollar fine levied by the court. It also filed a lawsuit, which eventually led to a U.S. Supreme Court ruling that the organization had a constitutional right to refuse to disclose the names of its members.[1] Forced disclosure of the membership list would infringe upon the First Amendment's guarantee of "freedom of association," said the Supreme Court.

"Effective advocacy of both public and private points of view, particularly controversial ones, is undeniably enhanced by group association," the Court affirmed in its 1958 decision. Saying that there is a "close nexus between the freedoms of speech and assembly," the Court said, "it is beyond debate that freedom to engage in association for the advancement of beliefs and ideas is an inseparable aspect of the 'liberty' assured by the Due Process Clause of the Fourteenth Amendment, which embraces freedom of speech."

While the political movement for equal rights for LGBT people is different in many ways from that of African Americans and other racial minorities,[2] some forms of discrimination faced by African Americans have been parlayed against sexual minorities, too.

During the 1950s and even decades later, some states had laws that made it illegal for more than three gay people to gather together in public. The supposed justification for restricting this First Amendment right was to protect the public against "immoral conduct." Also during the 1950s, the U.S. government launched a widespread campaign to rid itself of Communists and "homosexuals." The U.S. Civil Service Commission fired gays, regardless of the quality or importance of their work, again claiming it did so because gay people were guilty of "immoral conduct" and might be subject to blackmail.

Eventually, federal courts began to scrutinize and call a halt to such claims. In 1969, for instance, the U.S. Court of Appeals for the District of Columbia ruled, in *Norton v. Macy,* that it was unlawful for the U.S. government to fire a budget analyst after he was arrested for meeting another man in public and inviting him back to his apartment.

"The notion that it could be an appropriate function of the federal bureaucracy to enforce the majority's conventional codes of conduct in the private lives of its employees is at war with elementary concepts of liberty, privacy, and diversity," wrote the appeals court.[3]

As the justification of "immoral conduct" began to fall away, the Federal Bureau of Investigation (FBI) used the excuse of "national security" to justify sending undercover officers to infiltrate meetings of gay activists and to collect the names and photos of gay people.[4]

Even as this book was being written, documents were emerging that indicated the federal government, through the Department of Defense (DOD) and other agencies, has been conducting surveillance of LGBT groups that protest the military's policy on gays in the military.[5] How can this keep happening, if the U.S. Constitution guarantees that the government will "make no law...abridging...*the right of the people peaceably to assemble*"?

As with the right to freedom of speech, the right to peaceably assemble has some limitations. Just like you can't yell "Fire!" in a crowded theater, you can't hold your gay-straight alliance meeting in the middle of the Golden Gate Bridge. But what if you want to hold your gay-straight alliance meetings at school? What if you want to attend a meeting of a nongay school group and its members won't let you?

Constitutional, statutory, and administrative laws can come into play in these instances, and at the federal, state, and local levels. Take the case of a group of students at White County High School, situated in the northeastern corner of Georgia.[6] In January 2005 these students sought to form a gay-straight alliance. They were going to call it PRIDE (Peers Rising in Diverse Education) and their purpose was to give support to students who "have been bullied or harassed because of their identity.... In particular... to support students who are lesbian, gay, bisexual, or transgender."[7]

Group organizer Kerry Pacer met with the high school principal, Bryan Dorsey, and asked that the group be officially recognized. Dorsey refused to recognize the group.

The students didn't give up, and continued to talk with the principal and also the superintendent of the county's schools, Paul Shaw, who eventually agreed to their request. However, in agreeing to recognize the group, Shaw told the students that they would have to submit to the principal a list of the group's members. The group, not knowing what its rights were, did submit such a list, but two months later, Dorsey asked the school board to create a new policy eliminating all non-curriculum-related clubs from the high school. The board approved the recommendation, and PRIDE's permission to meet was revoked.

But PRIDE members noticed that something was amiss. Even though non-curriculum-related clubs were no longer supposed to meet at the school, some were still doing so—such as a prayer group and the Shotgun Club. PRIDE filed a lawsuit in federal court.

The lawsuit's primary argument was that the high school's new policy violated PRIDE members' First Amendment right to the freedom to peaceably assemble, under both the U.S. Constitution and the Georgia Constitution. And, as is often the case with such lawsuits, a number of other legal issues were raised. In this case, for instance, the lawsuit charged violations of the First Amendment right to freedom of speech and the Fourteenth Amendment right to equal protection under both the U.S. and Georgia constitutions, and violation of the federal Equal Access Act.

The Equal Access Act is a federal statute passed by Congress in 1984 to make it easier for students to form religious groups in schools. But it's ended up becoming an important statute in protecting the right of gay-straight alliances to form in public schools.

The act states that:

> it shall be deemed unlawful for any public secondary school which receives federal financial assistance and which has a limited open forum to deny equal access or a fair opportunity to, or discriminate against, any students who wish to conduct a meeting within that limited open forum on the basis of the religious, political, philosophical, or other content of the speech at such meetings.[8]

Obviously, if you encounter resistance from school authorities while attempting to form a gay-straight alliance, the first things you'd want to know in deciding whether this federal statute applies to *your* school is:

• whether the school is public;
• whether it receives federal financial assistance;
• whether it has a "limited open forum."

Public schools are operated by the local or state government and are open to families who reside within the jurisdiction of that government. Nearly every public school receives some form of federal assistance, but to be sure, you can ask the local school committee or school board for a copy of its budget (it may be readily available on the board's Web site).

"Limited open forum" means that the school allows non-curriculum-related groups to meet on school premises during noninstructional time. It also means that:

• the meetings of the groups are student-initiated and that attendance is voluntary;
• neither the school nor the government sponsor or fund the group's
activities;
• while a teacher may be at the meeting, he or she is not a partici-
pant;
• the meetings do not interfere with educational activities at the
school;
• no one other than students of the school may direct or control the
group's activities;
• no one other than students of the school may "regularly attend" activities of the group.

While many schools readily accept gay student groups as part of
their overall student community, others do not.

In Colorado, for instance, school officials rejected a request by a
group of students at Palmer High School to form a gay-straight alliance
group in 2005. The students filed suit in federal court,[9] but before the case
could be heard, this school district also changed its rules governing student groups. The new policy stipulated that the only groups which could
be recognized by the schools were those related to curricula; because of
the new policy, a federal judge ruled in favor of the school district.

But in the White County case, a federal court judge ruled that, even
though the White County High School had changed its policy, it had
failed to enforce that policy uniformly.[10] Therefore, said the judge, the
school was still operating with a limited open forum and thus was prohibited by the Equal Access Act from discriminating against the gay-
straight alliance.

(Having found that the school officials had violated the federal law,
the court did not have to determine whether it also violated the various
constitutional rights of the students. But if the court had found that the
school did *not* violate the Equal Access Act, those other rights, including the First Amendment freedom to peaceably assemble, would have
become critical for the formation of the gay-straight alliance.)

Meanwhile, public officials hostile to the formation of gay-straight alliances are coming up with new ways to thwart the groups. Following the federal court ruling, White County School District officials approved a new policy requiring that students get their parents' permission to participate in a school club. And the Georgia General Assembly passed a bill requiring schools to make parents aware of what clubs their children might join and give them the option of designating which clubs their children may *not* join.[11]

In a similar case, a county school board in Kentucky agreed to an out-of-court settlement to allow a gay-straight alliance to form and to provide three hours of training to staff and students to help prevent future discrimination based on sexual orientation. But after a federal court accepted the agreement, the school board provided parents with an opportunity to have their children opt out of the sensitivity training, nearly half of students were able to avoid the "mandatory" training, and the program included only about thirty minutes of sexual-orientation information.[12]

The Idaho House of Representatives passed a bill in April 2006 to require that public school students get their parents' signature to join any school club or organization. The bill was aimed at discouraging the formation of a proposed gay-straight alliance at a high school in the House bill sponsor's district.[13]

Outside a school setting, Americans also have a right to "assemble" with whomever they want whenever they want, but, like with free speech, the government is allowed to put limits on gatherings for two reasons—if, as we discussed, they present dangers or if they violate the rights of others.

Crossing Rights

Not *everything* an LGBT person wants to do has to do with being lesbian, gay, bisexual, or transgender. Often the subjects and activities we're interested in have nothing to do with sex or sexual orientation. Surprisingly, this is where the law has been least helpful.

Take the rather notorious example of the Boy Scouts. Tim Curran, an Eagle Scout from California, was the first to challenge the group's policy of barring gays. After he turned eighteen and was too old to be a scout, Tim applied to become an assistant scoutmaster. The following summer, he was interviewed by the *Oakland Tribune* for an article about gay teens. The article didn't say anything about Tim's participation in the Boy Scouts, but when scout officials saw it, they informed him that they couldn't accept his application to be a scoutmaster.

Tim sued in state court, charging that the action of scout officials violated California's Unruh Civil Rights Act, according to which:

> all persons within the jurisdiction of this state are free and equal, and no matter what their sex, race, color, religion, ancestry, national origin, disability or medical condition are entitled to the full and equal accommodations, advantages, facilities, privileges, or services in all business establishments of every kind whatsoever.

Although the Unruh Act did not explicitly prohibit sexual-orientation discrimination when Tim pressed his lawsuit (between 1981 and 1998), state courts had construed it to include sexual orientation.[14]

Sometimes, however, courts choose to resolve cases without addressing the primary issues involved. And in Tim's case, the California Supreme Court resolved it—in favor of the Boy Scouts—simply by declaring that it did not consider the organization to be a "business establishment" and, therefore, that it was not subject to the state civil rights law.[15]

Because Tim's lawsuit had challenged the Boy Scouts' policy based only on state law, the ruling applied only within that state. Meanwhile, another Eagle Scout, James Dale, had begun to challenge the Boy Scouts exclusionary policy, too, and this time the lawsuit challenged it based on a state human rights law in New Jersey.

State human rights laws have become very important to LGBT people and other minorities who are frequent victims of discrimination, increasingly so in recent years.[16] Sixteen states and the District of Columbia prohibit discrimination based on sexual orientation in a wide variety of arenas, including employment, housing, public accommodations, education, and credit.[17] Because there are no similar comprehensive protections through federal law,[18] these state laws are often the only defense to protect an LGBT person from discrimination in many of these areas.

It was the human rights law of New Jersey—what the state calls the "Law against Discrimination"—that came to James Dale's rescue. The New Jersey Supreme Court ruled that the Boy Scouts violated the state law's prohibition of sexual-orientation discrimination in *public accommodations* when it revoked his membership after learning from a newspaper article that he was gay.

Usually when you hear the term "public accommodations," you think of things like buses or trains, hotel rooms, and restaurants. Each state law has its own definition of the term, and in New Jersey it includes a long list of places that accommodate the public. In brief, the Web site of the New Jersey Attorney General's Office summarizes it as including "any place that offers goods, services and facilities to the general public, such as a restaurant, hotel, doctor's office, camp, or theater."

Where does the Boy Scouts group come in? The New Jersey court found that the Boy Scouts sought membership from a population of people broad enough that it constituted the "general public," and that the group had a long history of working with various public entities and public service organizations.

The court ruled that the state human rights law was based on an important rationale—eliminating discrimination based on sexual orientation—and that the law did not infringe on the Boy Scouts organization's freedom of association because "there is nothing to suggest that one of [the organization's] purposes is to promote the view that homosexuality is immoral."

Here again, the ruling would have applied only to New Jersey, but the Boy Scouts appealed to the U.S. Supreme Court. There, the organization argued that requiring the Boy Scouts to allow gay people to participate in its activities violated its First Amendment right to freedom of association. And the U.S. Supreme Court agreed.

"The forced inclusion of an unwanted person in a group infringes the group's freedom of expressive association if the presence of that person affects in a significant way the group's ability to advocate public or private viewpoints," wrote Chief Justice William Rehnquist, for himself and four other justices who joined him in the majority opinion. While noting that the First Amendment could be overridden "to serve compelling state interests, unrelated to the suppression of ideas," the majority said that New Jersey's interests in eradicating discrimination based on sexual orientation did not justify "such a severe intrusion on the Boy Scouts' rights to freedom of expressive association."[19]

The U.S. Supreme Court ruling, of course, applies everywhere in the country, so the decision in *Boy Scouts v. Dale* was a blow for LGBT people everywhere. It was so not because LGBT people everywhere are clamoring to join the Boy Scouts, but because the Supreme Court ruling seriously undermined the strength of state laws that prohibit discrimination.

The *Boy Scouts of America* decision also cracked open a door to allow groups that want to discriminate against LGBT people to try and slip past antidiscrimination laws, too. All a group had to do, according to the Court, was "engage in some form of expression" that would be undermined by the presence of gays. For the Boy Scouts, it was adequate that the organization's stated form of expression was to "instill values in young people" and that those values included being "morally straight" and "clean."

Dozens of lawsuits have been filed in federal courts around the country in recent years, seeking exemptions to various nondiscrimination laws protecting LGBT people. In Pennsylvania, a parent challenged a school's policy against hate speech, saying that, as Christians, his children are taught that homosexuality is a sin and should have a right to say so in school.[20] Many of the challenges have been to nondiscrimination policies on college campuses. Echoing the reasoning of the U.S.

Supreme Court, many of these religious groups claim that they are not discriminating against LGBT people but are simply excluding people who do not share their belief that homosexuality is a sin.[21]

In July 2006, the Seventh Circuit U.S. Court of Appeals agreed. Citing the *Boy Scouts v. Dale* opinion from the Supreme Court, a three-judge panel of the Seventh Circuit ruled that the freedom to peaceably assemble under the First Amendment protected the Christian Legal Society campus group at Southern Illinois University from having to admit LGBT members even though the university had a policy of banning discrimination based on sexual orientation.[22] The circuit panel also stated that the Christian group could not be found guilty of violating the university's nondiscrimination policy, because the group's rules concerning membership were "based on [religious] belief and ['homosexual conduct'] behavior rather than status [sexual orientation]."

10

When Your Life
Is On the Line

In one of the worst cases of antigay harassment ever documented in a public school, a middle school student restrained an openly gay student, Jamie Nabozny, on the floor of his seventh-grade science class while, with twenty classmates looking on and laughing, another student simulated raping him.

When Jamie broke free and ran to the principal's office for help, Principal Mary Podlesny brushed off the incident as an example of how "boys will be boys" and suggested that Jamie's openness about being gay prompted the event. She took no action against the assailants and no action to protect Jamie from further abuse.

Jamie experienced similar incidents throughout middle school and into high school in his rural Wisconsin community, including assaults in the boys' bathroom in which other boys urinated on him. Despite repeated requests for help from Jamie and his parents, school officials did nothing. After an incident in which a group of students repeatedly kicked Jamie in the stomach, Jamie sought to press charges against the students, but a police liaison to the school discouraged him from doing so. The assaults continued, and even after Jamie attempted suicide, a school counselor informed his parents that school officials intended to do nothing to protect him.

Jamie left Ashland, Wisconsin, and moved to Minneapolis. But rather than try to forget what had happened to him, Jamie sought legal help and filed a lawsuit in federal court against the Ashland school officials. The lawsuit charged that, by failing to take any action to stop the attacks against Jamie, the school principal and other officials violated his Fourteenth Amendment rights to equal protection and due process under the U.S. Constitution.

The Fourteenth Amendment, as discussed earlier, came about in an effort to secure equal rights for African Americans who had been freed as a result of the Civil War but who still faced considerable discrimination for decades thereafter. While the amendment does a number of things, its most prominent provisions are these:

> All persons born or naturalized in the United States, and subject to the jurisdiction thereof, are citizens of the United States and of the State wherein they reside. No State shall make or enforce any law which shall abridge the privileges or immunities of citizens of the United States; nor shall any State deprive any person of life, liberty, or property, without due process of law; nor deny to any person within its jurisdiction the equal protection of the laws.[1]

Why equal protection? School officials had a legal obligation to protect *all students* from harassment, and thus that obligation extended to Jamie too. And due process? Jamie had a reasonable expectation that school officials would treat his attackers as they treated other students who engaged in such activity (that they would punish them with expulsion). Because they did nothing, they failed to observe the ordinary procedures—due process—that they had followed in similar situations involving nongay students.

A U.S. district court judge dismissed Jamie's lawsuit. But whenever a lawsuit is dismissed—or thrown out of court—the person who filed it can appeal that dismissal to the next highest court. With the help of Lambda Legal Defense and Education Fund, Jamie appealed to the Seventh Circuit U.S. Court of Appeals. There, a three-judge panel ruled that Jamie had a legitimate claim that school officials had failed to administer to him equal protection of the law.[2] The Seventh Circuit sent the case back to a federal jury, and after a two-day trial the jury found the school officials guilty of violating Jamie's right to equal protection.

After losing a case on its legal arguments, the losing party can appeal a decision to the next highest level, too. But rather than appeal the decision, the Ashland School District agreed to pay Jamie nine hundred thousand dollars in damages and settle the legal conflict out of court.

Jamie's victory, said Lambda, sent a powerful message to other school districts that the price of ignoring harassment against gay students would be high.

It would be nice to think that that message got through to every school district in the country, or that Jamie's was an isolated case. But harassment is still one of the most pervasive problems for sexual-minority youth. As we saw in an earlier chapter, a national survey of students thirteen to eighteen years of age, conducted in January 2005, found that 65 percent of those surveyed had been harassed at school for some reason—whether it was their religion, race, sexual-minority status, or gender. Sixty-nine percent said they frequently heard other students use the phrase "That's so gay" as a derogatory remark, and 52 percent said they "frequently" heard other specifically antigay remarks from students.[3]

A survey in 2003 by the Gay, Lesbian, & Straight Education Network (GLSEN) found that more than 80 percent of students who identified as gay, lesbian, bisexual, or transgender reported being verbally harassed in school.[4] Seventy-five percent reported feeling unsafe in school because of their sexual orientation or gender expression. And over one-third had experienced some form of physical harassment because of their sexual orientation.

The GLSEN survey, completed by 308 sexual-minority students in middle school or high school, also indicated that fear of being assaulted had prompted almost one-third of these sexual-minority students to skip school during the previous month. Students who were subjected to frequent verbal harassment reported having lower grade point averages than students who had not been subjected to harassment.

Laws exist to protect such students, yet only about half of those who said they were harassed or assaulted reported the incidents to school authorities. Even fewer reported them to their families. Of those students who did tell their parents about being harassed or assaulted because of their sexual orientation, 20 percent said their parents took no action to contact school authorities about the incidents.

Sometimes you might think the best way to handle harassment or the violation of your rights is to just try and ignore it. Maybe it seems easier to endure the torment than it does to tell a parent or school official that you're being harassed as "gay." Maybe graduation is just months away, and you figure you can get through it and then, once you're out of school or turn eighteen, you can escape by moving to a place where being gay or lesbian, bisexual or transgender, is easier.

Unfortunately, the failure of victims to take action against wrongdoing often emboldens harassers, making things worse for the victim and for others. And the truth is: There is no totally safe haven. Even the friendliest of cities report problems. The FBI reported 1,017 hate-crime incidents based on antigay, anti-lesbian, or anti-bisexual sentiment in 2005.[5] The city with the largest number of LGBT-related hate crimes (47) was San Francisco. Boston, capital of the most LGBT-friendly state in the country, registered 26—more than a third of the state's total. A surprising number of hate crimes centered on college campuses— Brown University registered 5 of Rhode Island's 7 gay-related hate crimes. Universities in Pennsylvania accounted for 15 of the state's 18 gay-related hate crimes (with 12 of them on one campus—West Chester University[6]).

But there are state and federal laws to stop harassment, and many places you can go for help in making those laws work for you and protecting you from having your rights trampled on. Learning how to harness those laws and how to respond appropriately can often stop the harassment in its tracks and create a safer environment for you and others.

Laws in Schools

Derek Henkle did that in Reno, Nevada, against enormous odds. His problems began developing after he agreed to talk on a local cable access program about his experience as a gay student in high school. At first he was harassed with a barrage of verbal antigay slurs from classmates at school. Then things quickly escalated.

"In the middle of my school parking lot, a group of six students surrounded me and pulled up a lasso and said, 'Let's string up the fag and drag him down the highway,'" recalled Derek. "They got the lasso around my neck three times."[7]

Although Derek escaped and used a phone inside the school building to call the principal's office for help, no one came to his assistance for more than an hour. During that time, he had to hide in a nearby classroom. Finally, when assistant principal Denise Hausauer did arrive and Derek told her what had happened, Hausauer laughed and school officials took no action against Derek's attackers.

Instead, Derek was transferred, in the fall of 1995, to another high school, but the environment there was not much better. In fact, a school district official instructed him to keep his sexual orientation private and the school's principal told him to stop acting like a "fag." Derek was soon transferred to a third high school. At this school, a group of students attacked Derek, punching him in the face until he bled, while two county police officers "were present at the scene but deliberately, purposefully and intentionally took no action" to help Derek or stop his attackers.[8]

"When school officials constantly switched me from school to school, they said they were trying to keep me safe," said Derek. "In fact, they didn't care about me at all, they just wanted to sweep the abuse under the rug. Gay and lesbian kids should be able to be who they are, and free to pursue an education in a safe and supportive environment."[9]

Like Jamie, Derek fought back in federal court with a lawsuit filed by Lambda Legal Defense and Education Fund in January 2000. The lawsuit made a number of charges, both state and federal, constitutional and common law. Among those were claims that school officials had, by failing to protect him, violated Derek's U.S. constitutional right to equal protection, based on sex, and that they had violated the federal Civil Rights Act.[10] Neither of these laws prohibits discrimination based on sexual orientation. However, just two years earlier, the U.S. Supreme Court had ruled that a man who had been harassed by male employees with physical assaults in a sexual manner had been the victim of *discrimination based on sex* even though the perpetrators and the victim were of the same sex.[11]

In 2002 Derek won $451,000 in damages in a settlement with his school district. The settlement, said Lambda, was "the first to recognize the constitutional right of lesbian and gay youth to be out at school and protected from harassment."

Even more important, Derek won an agreement from the school district to make improvements in how school officials treat LGBT students and how they protect them. Among other things, the school district agreed to train its staff on how to prevent and stop harassment of LGBT students, to widely post notice of its policy banning discrimination based on sexual orientation, and to allow LGBT students to speak freely about their sexual orientation.

"The message has gone out to our administrators and staff: Any kid, gay or straight, rich or poor, black or white...who sets foot on our school has a right to be treated with dignity, respect and free of harassment," said Steve Mulvenon, communications director for the school district, in an interview with the *San Francisco Chronicle*. "Schools should be safe havens for all kids."[12]

Schools should be safe havens, and many are; but whether you're an LGBT youth or not, you need to be aware that antigay "harassment" can be aimed at anyone and that common verbal harassment can quickly turn into a hate crime and sometimes into murder.

Thirteen-year-old Josh Belluardo was riding the school bus home from his middle school in Woodstock, Georgia, on November 2, 1998, when an older student began taunting him with antigay slurs in front of other students on the bus. There was no indication that Josh was gay; one witness said he was the target that day simply because he had a new haircut.

"Josh never said a thing to him," said one witness. But the fifteen-

year-old threatened to beat Josh and said gay people deserved to die. After Josh stepped off the bus, the older teen struck him on the back of the
head; when Josh fell to the ground, the attacker began kicking him in
the stomach and the face. Josh's fifteen-year-old sister and a neighbor
rushed to Josh's aid, but the youngster was already unconscious. Forty-
eight hours later, he was dead.[13]

Josh's death, and that of another young teen who was bullied,
prompted the Georgia legislature to pass a law in 1999 to create programs in public schools aimed at discouraging and punishing bullying.[14] While the Georgia law does not specifically mention harassment
based on sexual orientation, similar laws passed by other states do.[15] For
instance, in Vermont, the law requires school boards to develop programs to stop harassment based on a variety of factors, including sexual
orientation.

Even if your state does not have an antibullying law, there are federal statutes that provide incentives for school officials to stop harassment and that may provide you with additional recourse if they don't.
We've discussed one before: Title IX of the Education Amendments of
1972. Title IX prohibits sex discrimination in any school that receives
federal funding. There's nothing in that law about "sexual orientation"
or "antigay," or anything LGBT. But after the law was passed, the Office
of Civil Rights in the Department of Education had the task of writing
the regulations—the administrative law—on how the law would be enforced. Courts had ruled that sex discrimination includes sexual harassment and, when the office revised its regulations in 1997, it said that
sexual harassment also includes sexual-orientation harassment.

Also, the Safe and Drug-Free Schools and Committees Act,[16] enacted in January 2002, calls for the U.S. Department of Education to
make grants to local educational agencies and community-based organizations to implement programs and training for students and staff to
help prevent and reduce hate crimes in "schools and communities."

Keep in mind that bullying is not something that only LGBT students face. In a report on crimes at schools in 2003, 12 percent of stu-

dents age twelve to eighteen reported having been called a hate-related name. Of that 12 percent, 4 percent were called race-related hate words, more than 2 percent each concerned gender or ethnicity, and more than 1 percent each concerned religion, disability, or sexual orientation.[17]

It's a big enough and common enough problem that, even if you haven't experienced it yourself, you may want to take some action before something happens. Check to see if your state has passed a law mandating that all public schools develop a program to prevent bullying. Then, find out if your school has such a program in place. If not, consider urging your school's principal to develop one.

And remember this: Regardless of whether your school has a policy in place to deal with harassment, it is a crime for someone to attack you. What's the difference between harassment and hate crime?

"There is no bright line between hate crime and noncriminal harassment, and some incidents may include elements of both," stated a 1999 publication released by the U.S. Department of Education and the National Association of Attorneys General. Generally speaking, according to this publication, hate crimes involve a crime in which the victim has been deliberately "selected based on characteristics such as race, national origin, ethnicity, sex/gender, religion, sexual orientation or disability."

"Typical hate crimes," according to the publication, "include threatening phone calls, hate mail, physical assault, threats of harm or violence, arson, vandalism, cross burnings, destruction of religious symbols, bombings and bomb threats."[18]

While the term "assault" has a different definition under each state's criminal code, generally speaking all states make it a crime for someone to deliberately touch you in any way that is intended to cause you harm, regardless of whether an actual physical injury occurs. And it is a crime to threaten you verbally in such a way as to make you believe the person can and will inflict bodily harm against you. Criminal laws apply both in and out of schools.

Out-of-School Experience

Of course, not all harassment is limited to schools. In fact, most hate-motivated crimes against LGBT people take place outside of school and most seem aimed at young people.[19] Some of the cases have become subjects of widespread publicity and are well known—like the case of Matthew Shepard, a twenty-one-year-old Wyoming man who was offered a ride by two male youths at a bar, taken to an isolated area, and beaten to death. Brandon Teena was also twenty-one and, though born with the body of a female, was living as a man; Brandon was raped, then shot and killed while at home in Nebraska. The attackers in both of those cases were caught and prosecuted.

But most victims of hate crimes are not well known, and sometimes their attackers are never found.

Sakia Gunn, fifteen, was with a group of girlfriends at a bus stop in Newark, New Jersey. They were on their way home from a night on the town May 11, 2004. As they waited for a bus, two men pulled up in a station wagon and asked them if they wanted to go have some "fun." When the girls replied, "No, we're gay," the men became angry, jumped out of the car, and attacked the girls. One of the men stabbed Sakia. She bled to death before her friends could get her to a hospital.[20]

Timothy Blair Jr., nineteen, was found shot to death in Louisville, Kentucky, in May 2005. According to his mother, he was gay; she believes that Timothy's sexual orientation, and the fact that he was a black man and dressed in drag, is why police never found his killer.[21]

Dwan Prince, a twenty-seven-year-old construction worker in Brooklyn, New York, was taking out his garbage one night in 2005 when Steven Pomie walked by wearing a woman's pink tank top. Dwan made some flirtatious remark to Pomie, and Pomie began yelling antigay slurs and beating and kicking him. Though Pomie was convicted and sentenced to twenty-five years in prison, Dwan was severely brain-damaged and is not able to work or take care of himself.[22]

So, as you can see, antigay hate crimes can victimize almost anyone

—regardless of whether they have self-identified as an LGBT person and even when they do not even appear to be LGBT.

Unfortunately, laws around hate crimes are more reactive than proactive. Their purpose is to discourage hate crimes but they do so only by administering a harsher sentence to someone who has already committed an assault. And the law gets at only those perpetrators who have been successfully prosecuted and convicted. And few state hate-crimes laws include harsher penalties when the assault has been motivated by hatred for someone because of their gender identity.

The U.S. Congress has included sexual orientation in few laws addressing hate crimes.[23] It passed a law in 1990 to simply gather statistics on such crimes.[24] But bills have been introduced to add sexual orientation and gender identity to a federal statute that allows the federal government to investigate and prosecute hate crimes.

According to the FBI, a hate crime is a "criminal offense committed against a person, property, or society that is motivated, in whole or in part, by the offender's bias against a race, religion, disability, sexual orientation, or ethnicity/national origin."[25] In a recent annual report on hate-crime statistics, the FBI reported that hate crimes based on sexual orientation are the third most frequent type of hate crime in the United States. While most hate crimes (54.7 percent) are based on race, hate crimes based on a person's religion and sexual orientation account for 17.1 percent and 14.2 percent respectively.[26]

Some critics of hate-crime laws argue that they are unconstitutional because they punish a person for what he or she thinks. But criminal law already takes motive into account when defining assaults. An "aggravated assault," for instance, is treated more harshly than a "simple assault" because of the perception that in the former, the assailant deliberately harmed someone, demonstrating an extraordinary lack of concern about the injury he or she would inflict on that person.

In a hate crime, the motive is to attack more than just the person who is the victim of the physical assault by making sure the attack conveys a threatening message to everyone who sees or hears about it that the assailant, for example, "hates all fags" or "hates all queers." Such attacks not only have a destructive impact on the individual victim, they inflict an injury upon the community's sense of safety generally and send a more specific threat to everyone in the community who is LGBT or even feels different in some other way.

What to Do

If harassment or a hate crime takes place at school, on a school bus, or during school-related activities, the most important thing to do, says Lambda Legal Defense and Education Fund, is to report the abuse—to the school principal, if you're being harassed at school, and/or to local police.

"No school can take action if it does not know about an abuse problem," according to Lambda.[27] And if you fail to inform officials, they are less likely to be held liable for not taking action to protect you.

The U.S. Department of Education suggests that students victimized at school report the incident to police; the department emphasizes, however, that just because you report an incident to the police "does not relieve the school district of its obligation to investigate, make findings, and remedy the harassment insofar as school-related conduct is involved."[28]

Because verbal abuse often escalates to physical abuse, notes Lambda, it's also important to report "all forms of abuse."

And while it's important to report the abuse to the appropriate official *in person*, you should then reiterate your complaint *in writing* to that person and keep a copy of it. In fact, document every contact you have with the official and keep notes about how they respond to you. The written complaint, says Lambda, should include:

- the "key details of the abuse, such as who, what, when, where";
- a list of any witnesses who saw what happened and, if possible, written statements from each of those witnesses about what they saw (be sure to make copies of these for your file, too);

• "details of any verbal exchange with the principal," noting, for instance, when you talked to the principal, what he or she said, and when he or she promised to get back to you.

Lambda emphasizes that some actions by the principal may be inappropriate and actually make the abuse worse. "It is inappropriate for the school to change the class schedule or seating assignment of the abused student, as if she or he, instead of the misbehaving student, is the problem," says Lambda. "Such responses can make matters worse because they make it clear to abusive students that the abuse is to be expected, and that the gay-identified student is not worthy of meaningful actions by the school officials."[29]

If a principal takes no action, inappropriate actions, actions that are insufficient in stopping the abuse, or fails to take action swiftly enough to stop continued abuse, you should take your complaint to the next highest level—usually the superintendent of your school district. After that, the next levels are usually the local school board or school committee, and then the head of the state department of education.

Lambda also suggests letting supportive organizations know of your situation, such as your school's gay-straight alliance or parent-teacher organization, the local chapter of Parents, Families, and Friends of Lesbians and Gays, or the Gay, Lesbian & Straight Education Network.

If you are the victim of a hate crime outside of school or school-related activities, you should:

• call the police immediately and request medical assistance, if needed;
• do not disturb any evidence, such as graffiti, objects used in the attack, threatening messages, etc.;
• make note of the exact words spoken to you during the attack;
• record the names and descriptions of your attackers, and any vehicle they may have been traveling in, along with license plate number;

• write down the names and contact information of any other victims and witnesses to the attack;
• contact any local organization that works to stop hate crimes.[30]

Additionally, the New York City Gay & Lesbian Anti-Violence Project offers these tips to help you avoid becoming the victim of a hate crime:

• Be aware of and avoid local "danger zones" where anti-LGBT attacks have been reported.
• Trust your instincts: If you feel like an attack is imminent, run, dial 911, yell "Fire!" bang garbage cans, or blow a whistle to draw attention to the scene.
• Don't let strangers into your home, and if you're getting ready to leave a bar with someone you have just met, first be sure to introduce that person to a friend, a bartender, or someone.
• Women: avoid using taxicabs that are waiting outside women's bars and be wary of men you don't know who claim to be gay and invite you to their homes.
• Travel in groups, particularly to bars, gay community centers, and gay events.[31]

11

Protecting Your Privacy

A recent survey asked lesbian, gay, and bisexual youth between the ages of fifteen and nineteen whether their parents knew they were gay. According to the results, 61 percent of the mothers and 54 percent of the fathers were believed to "definitely know." Twenty-four percent of the mothers and 34 percent of the fathers "definitely did *not* know," leaving 15 percent of moms and 12 percent of dads in some zone of "probably" does or doesn't know.[1]

This survey also asked the teens to assess their own sexual orientation, using the Kinsey Scale.[2] Twenty-three percent identified as being "totally gay or lesbian," 20 percent were "almost totally gay or lesbian," 21 percent were "bisexual but mostly gay or lesbian," 17 percent were "bisexual, but equally gay or lesbian and heterosexual," 19 percent were "bisexual but mostly heterosexual," and one youth identified as uncertain.

And believe it or not, there's also a psychological scale for quantifying how "gender typical" or "gender atypical" you are. The so-called Gender Conformity Scale asks how often during your early childhood (before you turned thirteen) you acted or thought in a manner that one might typically associate with your physical gender.[3] Like the Kinsey Scale, this scale ranges from zero to six, with zero being always conforming and six being always nonconforming. Most of the teens in the study landed somewhere in the middle.

Both boys and girls reported becoming aware of their same-sex attraction around age ten and telling their parents at about age fourteen. Those who tended not to conform to gender stereotypes as children were more likely to have told their parents about their sexual orientation than those who tended to conform.

"Parents' reactions were nearly equally split between positive and negative," said the study, regardless of whether they were reacting to a son's or a daughter's sexual orientation. For instance, 55 percent of mothers were either "positive or very positive" about their son's being gay and 45 percent were "negative or very negative."

Regardless of whether it was mother reacting to son or daughter, or father reacting to son or daughter, 12 to 18 percent of parents had "very negative" responses to their child's being gay.[4]

The survey tells us two important things: More than one-third of the teens had parents who did not know they were lesbian, gay, or bisexual (LGB), and LGB teens don't necessarily signal their sexual orientation by acting in a gender-atypical way during childhood, and thus, "have been more able to avoid parental discovery of their sexual orientation."[5]

Now, imagine you're among these one in three teens whose parents *don't* know about your being LGBT, and you're riding along in the car with them one day. They're taking you to the family doctor to get your annual checkup when one of them says something like, "I want you to feel free to ask the doctor about, you know, whatever you might have questions about, OK?" That's their way of referring to "sex." And just because they want you to feel free to ask the doctor about sex does *not* mean they want you to *have* sex right now. In fact, surveys of parents show that 83 percent of them think having sex outside of marriage is a "sin," even though, at the same time, half *don't* think it's "morally wrong."[6] In other words, there's a good chance your parents don't know what to say to you but they know you need to know about sex.

Even if your parents are unusually resourceful and stumble upon the "Parent Package" put together by the American Medical Association on what health issues to talk to children about, it's a thirty-page booklet that mentions "gays or lesbians" only once and all it tells them is: "If your teen tells you that he or she is homosexual, he or she will need your love and support. You, in turn, may benefit from a support group for parents of gays and lesbians." That's not much to go on, especially if, as we've learned in the survey of LGB teens, parents don't have a clue about their children's sexual orientation. And let's face it, most parents today are probably more likely concerned about the possibility that you'll get pregnant or get someone else pregnant.

But you're riding in the car, and thinking about this, and you decide that you *do* have some questions you'd like to ask somebody. Maybe you're already having sex and you're not sure you're getting the condom on right. Maybe it broke once and you're afraid you have HIV. Maybe when you kissed your girlfriend the other night, you noticed a strange bump on her lip. She didn't know what it was and now you have one and you don't know what it is either. Maybe, since they don't discuss gay-specific information in your sex ed class, you want some facts about anal intercourse or using dildos. Can you trust your family doctor to keep your questions confidential? Can he or she give you an HIV test or treat a sexually transmitted disease without telling your parents?

While some of the answers are dependent on your doctor, a lot is dictated by law—both federal and state law.

If you're under eighteen, you're below the age of majority in most states, which means two things in this context: (1) you're not legally old enough to consent to medical treatment, and (2) your parents have a legal right to see your medical record and obtain information from your doctor about your health.

Does that mean the doctor has to tell your parents anything you say during your visit? If you ask about condoms, does the doctor have to get permission from your parents to give them to you? Maybe what you really want is to talk to a therapist about your feelings about being gay or your confusion about whatever your sexual orientation might be. Maybe, like too many sexual-minority youth, you've had thoughts about suicide.

A survey of 3,162 adolescent boys and 3,586 girls found that "the leading reason adolescents gave for not getting needed [medical] care was reluctance to tell their parents about their problem."[7] So, what are your rights to privacy in talking to a physician or therapist?

"Privacy is a shared assumption, a contract, and a core ethical principle in medicine, dating back to Hippocrates," asserts Patient Privacy

Rights Foundation, an organization that advocates on behalf of keeping patient information private. But it's not a reality. Not only might your parents have a right to know certain things that land in your medical records, so can a whole slew of other people—insurance company representatives, public health officials, pharmaceutical research groups, and others.

"Though your doctors are sworn to keeping your information private, once information is sent out of their offices, they have no control over how the information is used."[8] And recent changes in a federal law regarding privacy of medical records have reportedly made it easier for information to be shared with persons outside the doctor's office.

Congress passed a federal law, the Health Insurance Portability and Accountability Act (HIPAA),[9] in 1996, and in it included some provisions for ensuring the privacy of medical records. Then the U.S. Department of Health and Human Services (HHS) wrote the administrative laws—or regulations—to put the privacy law into force, in 2003. The privacy law regulations are known as the HIPAA Privacy Rule.

Generally speaking, as long as you are under the age of majority in your state, this federal law allows your parents to have access to your medical records. There are, however, two important exceptions to this rule: (1) "when such access is not inconsistent with State or other law," and (2) when a doctor believes that providing such access could harm you.

In the ironically titled 101-page "HIPAA Administrative Simplification Regulation Text," HHS states that:

> If under applicable law a parent . . . has authority to act on behalf of an individual who is an unemancipated minor in making decisions related to health care, a [health care provider] must treat such person as a personal representative . . . with respect to protected health information.[10]

A "personal representative" is a person who has the legal authority to act on your behalf. If you are under the age of majority, this is usually your parents or guardians and, as such, they are entitled to know what is in your medical record. However, in some states, state law allows a young person to seek medical treatment for certain matters without parental consent, and in those situations a doctor may not have to share this information with your parents.

You may also seek a court order for permission to seek certain treatment despite your parents' objections or without their consent. But the easiest legal option of all is for your parents to agree to instruct the doctor that your interactions with him or her be designated as confidential. If you're on good terms with your parents, this is the obvious first choice, and you may ask your doctor to suggest this option to your parents.

Sounds pretty good, right? Well, there is a loophole: Even if your parents are no longer your personal representative, your doctor or psychologist may, without your permission, disclose private information to them in some circumstances.

The regulations, explains Patrick D. Hadley, senior adviser, HIPAA Privacy Outreach at the U.S. Department of Health and Human Services' Office for Civil Rights, are written to accommodate a wide variety of situations. As an illustration, one scenario the law tries to provide for is one in which you are, say, nineteen, single, and in college. You haven't prepared a health proxy or power of attorney to give anyone else the right to make emergency health decisions for you, and you're injured in a car accident and in a coma. Although you are beyond the "age of majority," a doctor can, "in the exercise of professional judgment," share information about your condition with your parents. In most cases, this is probably what you would want.

There's another loophole that works the other way. Imagine you're under the age of majority—let's say sixteen—but you've left home and are living with your best friend's parents because your parents became physically and emotionally abusive after learning that you're gay. You haven't gone to court to obtain emancipation. Now, you're in a car accident and you're in a coma, but your best friend's parents warn the doctor that you've left home because your parents have been abusive. Your parents show up and, *legally,* they are your personal representative. A doctor may withhold information from your parents if he or she has "a reasonable belief" that:

- you have been "or may be subjected to domestic violence, abuse, or neglect" by your parents;
- "treating [your parents] as the personal representative could endanger" you.

In either of those circumstances, if the doctor decides that it is not in your best interest to allow your parents to make decisions as your personal representative, he or she may *refuse* to disclose information to them.[11]

So, to some extent, the confidentiality you enjoy with your doctor is largely dependent on his or her professional judgment about what's in your best interest.

In releasing the regulations, HHS included some explanations of how its regulations take this relationship between patient and doctor into account. And it explained how many people operate under assumptions about confidentiality that are simply untrue.

"Comments from individuals revealed a common belief that, today, people must be asked permission for each and every release of their health information. Many believe that they 'own' the health records about them. However, current law and practice do not support this view."[12]

Many health care practitioners follow guidelines adopted by their respective professional associations, such as the American Medical Association (AMA), says HHS, but these guidelines do not have the force of law.

"For example, the American Medical Association's Code of Ethics," notes HHS, "recognizes both the right to privacy and the need to balance it against societal needs." AMA's code suggests that if there is a conflict "between a patient's right to privacy and a third party's need to know" the conflict "should be resolved in favor of the patient, except where that would result in serious health hazard or harm to the patient or others."[13]

In other words, as the HHS regulations document notes, "Individuals' right to privacy in information about themselves is not absolute." There are laws that allow the reporting of the names of people with certain sexually transmitted diseases to public health officials to enable notification of their sexual partners and ensure they receive proper testing and treatment. So, even if you *don't* go see a doctor about a sexually transmitted disease, if one of your sexual partners is diagnosed with one, you may be contacted by the public health department. That's why some clinics—gay and public clinics—were quick to set up HIV test sites where people who feared they may have been infected could get tested anonymously. And such sites are still available for HIV testing.

And again, there are differences in confidentiality protections depending on what state you live in. For instance, federal law requires the reporting of all HIV infections to the U.S. Centers for Disease Control and Prevention (CDC), but it does not require that the name of each person with HIV be reported. Instead, each state can decide for itself whether to require names or an identifying number to make each report. So if you are diagnosed with HIV in one state, it may be that only an anonymous code number is reported to CDC, whereas if you're diagnosed in another state, your name may be reported. And such laws are frequently changing. A new law in California went into effect in 2006, requiring all health care providers and laboratories processing HIV tests to start reporting to local health departments the names of people who tested positive. And other states are also considering name reporting.[14]

Regardless of what the law is at the federal level or in any given state, the reality is that, once any information is written into your medical record—that, for instance, you have a same-sex sexual partner—there is some measure of risk that the information could be read by people you don't know or people you don't want to have that information. Organizations advocating for stronger privacy protections have documented numerous cases of both intentional and unintentional breaches of private medical confidentiality. In 1999, thousands of medical records that were in a database system of the University of Michigan Medical Center were inadvertently made available online while the staff was trying out some new software.[15] Three months later, the unshredded health insurance claim forms of thousands of patients in Connecticut blew off a truck onto an interstate highway as they were being carted off to the dump.[16] The North Dakota Supreme Court ruled in June 2006 that it was permissible for an emergency room physician to initiate drug tests on a patient who had been in an automobile accident and turn the results over to police without first obtaining permission from the patient.

"Courts have generally recognized a patient's right to recover damages from a physician for the unauthorized disclosure of medical information about the patient," said the North Dakota court. But another state law, it said, requires a physician treating a patient who has suffered some injury from physical trauma that the doctor "has reasonable cause to suspect was inflicted in violation of any criminal law of this state" to "as soon as practicable report the same to the sheriff or state's attorney of the county in which such care was rendered."[17]

So as you can see, there are any number of ways in which information you provide to a doctor—or which the doctor learns about—in the context of a confidential medical examination and discussion can become public. The answer is not to avoid doctors, but to be aware of the privacy risks and do what you can to improve your odds. One way of improving your odds, of course, is to choose a doctor who you feel you can trust. That may be tricky if you're still covered under your parents' health insurance and you are going to a doctor whom they have chosen.

"Reliance on health insurance coverage for confidential care can be problematic for an adolescent. The necessity for a parent to sign the insurance claim (in the case of private insurance), or to furnish the Medicaid or SCHIP [State Children's Health Insurance Program] card significantly limits the confidentiality of services," according to a position paper of the Society for Adolescent Health. "Furthermore, the diagnoses on billing statements when mailed to parents can also violate confidentiality."[18]

But if your level of trust in your current doctor is so low that you're not providing him or her with information about yourself that could be crucial to your health, it's time to consider asking your parents if you can choose your own doctor.

If that doesn't feel like an option for you, there are instances in which you can seek medical help without your parents' consent. In most states, you can receive medical assistance without parental consent in an emergency and, of course, if you are considered an emancipated minor (see Chapter 1). According to the American Academy of Family Physicians, "most states" have laws allowing minors to seek help independently for "reproductive health services leading to the diagnosis and treatment of sexually transmitted infections (STI) and the diagnosis of pregnancy." States also frequently allow minors to seek treatment without parental consent for sexual assaults, mental health issues, and substance abuse.[19] For instance, in Texas you can consent to medical treatment on your own if you are at least sixteen and live apart from your parent or guardian and manage your own financial affairs, or if you are seeking treatment for an infectious, contagious, or communicable disease that must be reported to the state or seeking treatment for substance abuse or addiction.[20] You can also consider visiting a local community health clinic that provides free or low-cost health services; in many cities, there are such clinics organized for and by the LGBT community.

Beyond a doctor's office, there are other records you would probably prefer to keep private, too. If, for instance, you've gone to talk to the school counselor about being gay or being harassed because somebody thinks you're LGBT, the school counselor has almost certainly made a note about your conversation. After you turn eighteen or enter college, your school records belong to you exclusively and can no longer be seen by anyone, not even your parents, without your permission. But until then, the federal Family Educational Rights and Privacy Act (FERPA) provides your parents or guardians with access to such records.[21]

FERPA allows your parents or guardians to see your records at school, to seek corrections to any incorrect notations in those records, and to control who else sees them. There are important exceptions in this law. For instance, the law does not allow your parents access to records that are made by a "physician, psychiatrist, or psychologist" at school who might be treating you, but that doesn't necessarily cover a school counselor. Before you reveal anything sensitive to a school counselor, you should ask whether their records of their conversations with you will be available to your parents.

There are state laws that control access to your records as a minor under the care of a mental health professional outside of school, and these vary from state to state. For instance, in Illinois, the Mental Health and Developmental Disabilities Confidentiality Act permits a parent or guardian to see the records of his or her child if that child is under twelve years of age.[22] The parent or guardian can see the records of an older child up until the age of eighteen if the child "does not object or if the therapist does not find that there are compelling reasons for denying the access."

There can be a compelling reason for a health care provider to breach their confidential relationship with you. Rules regarding confidentiality change if your health care provider has reason to believe you might try to harm yourself or commit suicide. And there are also laws in some states that require health care professionals to report any instance in which they believe a minor has been the victim of child abuse or sexual abuse.

Afterword
Passing the Bar

Some years ago, I was watching one of those many television drama series based on a law firm. It was an especially popular series with the gay community at the time because it was one of the first to include a regular gay character. The show did its small part to ease into the American conscience the reality that sexual-minority people exist and that we are capable of carrying on useful and interesting lives.

But in one episode, the show also did a lot to misinform the American public about civil rights laws. In that episode, a lawyer was speaking with a heterosexual client who wanted to sue his employer for having fired him for being straight. The lawyer explained—quite incorrectly—that laws prohibiting discrimination based on sexual orientation protect *only gay* people. That, of course, is not true. But unfortunately, many Americans believe that much of what they hear about the law on television dramas is factual.

As I hope you have learned in this book, law can be quite complicated, and it can be easily misunderstood and misapplied by the very people who are charged with seeing that it is properly enforced. That is especially true for laws that LGBT people depend on frequently—both because few people feel they have a need to understand such laws and because bias can interfere with their fair implementation of them.

Maybe you will never have an occasion to wield your understanding of the law in order to protect your rights as an LGBT person, but the results of many surveys suggest otherwise. If such an incident does arise, I hope that what you have learned in this book will help you.

And I hope you will remember this, too: The LGBT civil rights movement does not need you to fight every injustice that comes your way. It needs you to be wise and careful in choosing your battles. In doing so, you have a right and a responsibility to consider many factors—

including your future, your emotional and financial capacity for waging battle, even your safety.

But there are many organizations and individuals ready and able to help you, whether your battle is a legal one or more personal. Knowing your rights, understanding how laws work, and availing yourself of those resources will enable you to make the most important contribution you can make to the movement—and that is living a life that is well and happy and honest.

Acknowledgments

Never having gone to law school myself, I owe a great debt of gratitude to those who have been willing to guide me far enough into the labyrinth of logic and legalese that I might convey the law's most useful secrets to others. Chief among these noble sages have been, for many years, Chai Feldblum, a preeminent professor of constitutional law at Georgetown University and a former law clerk to U.S. Supreme Court justice Harry Blackmun, and Evan Wolfson, head of the national Freedom to Marry organization and one of the LGBT civil rights movement's most accomplished litigators. They may not have been able to save me from every error, but they have certainly enabled me to deliver to lay readers a much more coherent and enlightened analysis of the law than I could ever have hoped to provide on my own.

I owe similar gratitude to many other lawyers and legal scholars, too many to list here, for their contribution to what amounts to my homeschooled legal education. Those who personally tackled some of the many questions raised in my research for this book are Jon Davidson, Hayley Gorenberg, and David Buckel at Lambda; Matt Coles and Elizabeth Littrell at the ACLU; and Jody Marksamer and Courtney Joslin at the National Council for Lesbian Rights.

I thank my spouse, Sheilah McCarthy, also an attorney, for her unwavering confidence that I would not lose my way or my mind in tackling this challenge and for sharing illumination when my wit grew dim.

And a special thanks to Michael Bronski and Gayatri Patnaik, who put the proverbial pen and paper in front of me and challenged me to write this book.

Appendix A
How to Look Up a Law

Some laws are written in "legalese," and therefore hard to read, but many are quite easily understood. And because they are public documents, they are fairly easy to find, including online. The following is a summary of tips from the Legal Information Institute of Cornell Law School on how to look up various types of laws.

Constitutional Laws

Copies of the U.S. Constitution and each of the state constitutions are accessible online. Whether you're looking up something in the U.S. Constitution or a state constitution, the reference will look something like this:

U.S. Const., art. III, § 2, cl. 2.

This citation refers to the United States Constitution, Article III, Section 2, Clause 2. If you look at that section of the Constitution, you find the passage that some believe enables Congress to take certain laws out of the U.S. Supreme Court's jurisdiction:

... the supreme court shall have appellate jurisdiction, both as to law and fact, with such exceptions, and under such regulations as the Congress shall make.

Ohio Const., art. XV, § 11

This citation is to the Ohio Constitution's Article XV, Section 11, the recent constitutional amendment banning recognition of same-sex marriages or other legal status for same-sex relationships.

Statutes

Federal and state statutes are also available online. To access federal statutes, go to uscode.house.gov. State codes are often referred to simply as the state name plus "code," such as "California Codes," but they can have other names, such as the "Illinois Compiled Statutes" or "the Missouri Revised Statutes." The quickest way to find your state's code online is to go to findlaw.com, click on "Cases & Codes" and then "State Law." Then pick your state from the list. Citations for statutes look like this:

20 U.S.C. § 7906

This citation refers to Chapter 20 of the United States Code, Section 7906, a part of the education code that prohibits certain federal funds from being used to develop youth programs that would "encourage sexual activity, whether homosexual or heterosexual." State statutes can be a little more cryptic. For instance, unless you were familiar with state codes, you wouldn't know which state the *M* in the following abbreviation stood for.

23 M.G.L. § 11k

But if you plug it into an online search engine, you'll quickly discover that "M.G.L." stands for Massachusetts General Laws. Chapter 23, Section 11k, is a state law that says the state Department of Labor must ensure that any apprentice program licensed by the state does not discriminate based on a number of characteristics, including sexual orientation.

To find a local ordinance, go to findlaw.com, click on "Cases & Codes," and then "State Law." Choose your state and then scroll down until you find your city's code. If your city isn't listed, try using a search engine.

Below is a citation for the human rights law of Ann Arbor, prohibiting discrimination based on sexual orientation. It is one of the oldest laws in the country prohibiting sexual-orientation discrimination.

Ann Arbor, Mich., City Code Ch. 112, Ordinance No. 4-78

Appendix B
States with Laws Banning Sexual-Orientation Discrimination

The following is a list of states (and the District of Columbia) that have laws banning sexual-orientation discrimination, along with the year in which the law was enacted.

District of Columbia	(1977)
Wisconsin	(1982)
Massachusetts	(1989)
Connecticut	(1991)
Hawaii	(1991)
New Jersey	(1992)
Vermont	(1992)
California	(1992)
Minnesota	(1993)
Rhode Island	(1995)
New Hampshire	(1997)
Maryland	(2001)
New York	(2003)
New Mexico	(2004)
Maine	(2005)
Illinois	(2005)
Washington	(2006)

For a list of local ordinances prohibiting discrimination based on sexual orientation, visit the Web site of the National Gay and Lesbian Task Force (thetaskforce.com), and click on "The Issues," and then "Non-Discrimination."

Appendix C
Timeline of Legal Landmarks
in U.S. LGBT Law

1600s   As they settle into colonies in the New World, Europeans
         govern themselves with laws they are familiar with from their
         homelands, including religiously based laws prohibiting any
         nonprocreative sexual activity ("sodomy") outside of marriage.

1700s   Following the American Revolution and with growing separa-
         tion between church and state, sodomy laws are applied almost
         exclusively to cases involving assaults against children, sex in
         public, or prostitution, *not* same-sex sexual relations in pri-
         vate. As the ACLU's brief to the Supreme Court in *Lawrence v.*
         Texas would explain in 2003, "State governments began taking
         a much more hands-off attitude toward regulation of private
         sexuality."

1800s   As cities begin to multiply and attract larger populations, men
         who have sex with men become more visible. Especially after
         the Civil War ends in 1865, an industry of sex workers grows to
         cater to a growing population of men moving into urban areas
         without their families. This prompts greater enforcement of
         laws against nonprocreative sex and the adoption, by the fed-
         eral government, of a code of conduct for civil service em-
         ployees to bar from employment anyone who engages in
         "immoral" or "indecent" behavior.

1924   Though short-lived, the first known gay group in the United
         States forms in Chicago: The Society for Human Rights. The
         group's activities are ended within a month after members are

arrested and charged with violating a federal law against using the mail to distribute obscene material (in this case, a newsletter with political content). The charges were later dropped.

1940s At the end of World War II, the United States and the Soviet Union engage in a "Cold War" of distrust and a race for military superiority. The distrust in the U.S. manifests itself as a witch hunt for Communists within the federal government. But some in Congress also target "homosexuals"; Ohio congressman Cliff Clevenger expresses the belief that "Russia makes a practice of keeping a list of sex perverts in enemy countries" in order to blackmail them for state secrets (*Congressional Record* 96, Part 4, 81st Congress, 2nd Session, March 29–April 24, 1950, pp. 4527–28).

1950s Just after sex researcher Alfred Kinsey publishes data showing a much greater number of people engaging in same-sex sexual relations than previously believed, the federal government campaign to eliminate gay people from federal jobs is in full swing. Through administrative law, President Dwight Eisenhower, in 1953, aids the effort by issuing an executive order calling for dismissal from government employment of anyone found to engage in "immoral" conduct or "sexual perversion." With J. Edgar Hoover heading the Federal Bureau of Investigation (FBI) and U.S. Senator Joseph McCarthy fueling the public hysteria over Communist infiltration (and sexual "perversion"), a new gay political group begins organizing on the West Coast. The Mattachine Society's aim is to seek better treatment of gay people under the law.

1952 The Mattachine Society holds its first national convention, April 11, in Los Angeles. Estimates of attendance are put between 100 and 500.

1953   The FBI begins conducting "exhaustive and apparently illegal surveillance" of gay groups. This was not revealed publicly until September 1989 when the *San Francisco Chronicle* published an article by openly gay reporter Randy Shilts detailing two decades of FBI surveillance of the gay community. Shilts noted that FBI director Hoover sent a memo to the Justice Department when the surveillance ended in 1975, noting that the bureau had found no evidence of any gay groups having ties to Communists.

1955   The American Law Institute proposes a Model Penal Code that decriminalizes nonprocreative sex in private.

1958   The U.S. Supreme Court reverses a decision of lower federal courts that had declared *One* magazine, a publication for gay readers, to be pornographic. The high court's action enables the publication to be distributed through the mail.

1961   Illinois becomes the first state to adopt the American Law Institute's model code and eliminate its law prohibiting same-sex sexual relations.

1962   Having been fired from his federal job in 1958 for being gay, Franklin Kameny forms a Mattachine chapter in Washington, D.C.

1965   On April 17, Kameny and the Mattachine Society stage the first gay civil rights protest in front of the White House.

1969   On June 27, patrons of a gay bar called Stonewall in New York City fight back against police harassment and laws that prohibited gay people from gathering in public. Later that year, a federal commission, led by Evelyn Hooker, submits to the government a report indicating that many gay people lead generally well-adjusted lives.

1970   *One* magazine obtains a copy of the suppressed Hooker Report and publishes it. On May 18, a gay male couple in Hennepin County, Minnesota, apply for a marriage license and are turned down. Two other gay couples—one in Kentucky and one in Washington state—also apply for marriage licenses and are turned down.

1972   The U.S. Supreme Court dismisses the first lawsuit to reach the high court seeking equal rights in marriage for same-sex couples. The case, *Baker v. Nelson,* was pressed by a gay male couple in Minnesota.

1973   The American Psychiatric Association votes to change its diagnostic manual's entry for homosexuality, essentially removing it as a psychiatric disorder. The Seattle City Council approves the first law in the country to prohibit discrimination based on sexual orientation. (The law is limited to employment.)

1975   The U.S. Civil Service Commission amends its regulations, which had previously barred gay people from government jobs.

1977   Former beauty pageant queen Anita Bryant launches the first national systematic campaign to overturn laws prohibiting discrimination based on sexual orientation. The U.S. Supreme Court vacates a lower court decision, in *Singer v. U.S. Civil Service Commission,* which had allowed the firing of a civil service employee in Seattle for being openly gay. The high court said the lower courts had to reconsider the case in light of the civil service commission's change in regulations concerning openly gay employees.

1978   The U.S. Supreme Court refuses to hear an appeal from the University of Missouri, which had been ordered by a federal appeals court to grant recognition to a campus gay group. In *Ratchford v. Gay Lib,* the Eighth Circuit had ruled that the group had a First Amendment right to speech and association.

1980   The U.S. Supreme Court refuses to hear an appeal from Texas A&M University, which had also sought to block a gay group from forming on campus. The Fifth Circuit, too, said that denial of recognition violated the rights to speech and association.

1985   The U.S. Supreme Court refuses to hear an appeal from a schoolteacher in Ohio who was fired for being bisexual. Two justices—William Brennan and Thurgood Marshall—take the unusual tack of writing a dissent to the Court's refusal to hear the case, *Rowland v. Mad River,* saying they believed serious constitutional violations had been made in the firing of Marjorie Rowland. In a major victory for equal rights for gays in employment, the U.S. Supreme Court, in *NGTF v. Oklahoma,* overturned a law that prohibited gays from teaching jobs. NGTF, the National Gay Task Force, changes its name to its current form, National Gay and Lesbian Task Force, that same year.

1986   The U.S. Supreme Court, by a 5 to 4 vote, upholds a state law prohibiting sex between partners of the same sex. The decision, in *Bowers v. Hardwick,* represents a major setback in the gay civil rights movement's campaign for equal rights and is used against LGBT people for many years in a wide variety of contexts.

1989   In *Hopkins v. Price Waterhouse,* the U.S. Supreme Court rules that Title VII, prohibiting sex discrimination in employment, in the federal Civil Rights Act, includes a prohibition against discrimination based on sex stereotypes.

1995   The U.S. Supreme Court, in *Hurley v. GLIB,* rules that the organizers of a St. Patrick's Day parade in Boston had a First Amendment freedom-of-expression right to exclude an openly gay contingent from participating.

1996   In *Romer v. Evans,* the U.S. Supreme Court rules that a ballot measure aimed at eliminating all means by which gays could seek redress for sexual-orientation discrimination violated the U.S. Constitution's guarantee of equal protection.

1998   President Bill Clinton signs an executive order prohibiting discrimination based on sexual orientation in federal employment. The U.S. Supreme Court, in *Oncale v. Sundowner,* rules that Title VII of the Civil Rights Act, prohibiting sex discrimination in employment, includes a prohibition of sexual harassment perpetrated by someone against a victim of the same sex.

2000   The U.S. Supreme Court rules that the Boy Scouts of America has a constitutional right to exclude gay people and that its right trumps a state human rights law's aim to eliminate discrimination based on sexual orientation.

2003   In *Lawrence v. Texas,* the U.S. Supreme Court overrules its 1986 decision in *Bowers v. Hardwick,* and strikes down laws prohibiting private consensual same-sex sexual relations as a violation of the U.S. Constitution's promise of liberty under the Fourteenth Amendment.

        For the first time ever, a state supreme court—in Massachusetts—rules that the state constitution's promise of equal protection under the law applies to same-sex couples seeking marriage licenses. The case, *Goodridge v. Department of Health,* was brought by Gay & Lesbian Advocates & Defenders on behalf of couples in Massachusetts, but the political reaction—both negative and positive—reverberates around the country and the world. The court sets May 17, 2004, as the date by which time the state government must begin issuing licenses to same-sex couples.

2004   Legislative efforts to stop implementation of the *Goodridge* decision fail, and around the country, various other local government officials attempt to issue marriage licenses in their jurisdictions, too. Many of those—including six cases out of San Francisco—were still being litigated in courts around the country as of this book's writing. On May 17, 2004, the Massachusetts Supreme Judicial Court's 2003 ruling in *Goodridge* takes effect, and for the first time in the country's history, thousands of same-sex couples in a state obtain marriage licenses that carry the same benefits and responsibilities as marriage licenses issued to straight couples.

Appendix D
States with Laws against Bullying in Schools

Most of the anti-bullying laws in the states listed here do the same things: They mandate that public schools adopt a policy to prevent bullying and harassment, require that school officials post that policy and take other measures to prevent bullying and harassment, oblige teachers and staff to report instances of such harassment, and require school officials to take actions to stop the harassment. Many states also have laws against harassment outside the school setting. (The list was compiled using information provided by the National Conference of State Legislatures.)

Arkansas
Arizona
California
Colorado
Connecticut
Georgia
Idaho
Indiana
Illinois
Louisiana
Maine
Maryland
Mississippi
Missouri
New Hampshire
New Jersey
Nevada

New York
Oklahoma
Oregon
Rhode Island
South Carolina
Tennessee
Utah
Vermont
Virginia
Washington
West Virginia

Appendix E
Laws Frequently Cited in
LGBT Civil Rights Lawsuits

U.S. Civil Rights Act
Commonly referred to as "Section 1983"
U.S. Code Title 42, Chapter 21, Subchapter I, Section 1983
42 U.S.C. §1983

The text: "Every person who, under color of any statute, ordinance, regulation, custom, or usage, of any State or Territory or the District of Columbia, subjects, or causes to be subjected, any citizen of the United States or other person within the jurisdiction thereof to the deprivation of any rights, privileges, or immunities secured by the Constitution and laws, shall be liable to the party injured in an action at law, suit in equity, or other proper proceeding for redress, except that in any action brought against a judicial officer for an act or omission taken in such officer's judicial capacity, injunctive relief shall not be granted unless a declaratory decree was violated or declaratory relief was unavailable. For the purposes of this section, any Act of Congress applicable exclusively to the District of Columbia shall be considered to be a statute of the District of Columbia."

Layperson translation: Anyone acting on behalf of a government entity who denies a citizen any constitutional right can be held liable for damages done to that person as a result of that denial.

Importance to LGBT: Enables a person whose rights have been violated by a government player (this includes public school teachers and principals, police, public health officers, private contractors hired by the government, volunteers working for the government, etc.) to sue that individual for redress in federal court. It's not the same as suing your school or your town; rather, you are suing an individual who is acting "under the color" of the government.

Equal Access Act
U.S. Code Title 20, Chapter 52, Subchapter VIII, Section 4071
20 U.S.C. § 4071

The text: "It shall be unlawful for any public secondary school which receives Federal financial assistance and which has a limited open forum to deny equal access or a fair opportunity to, or discriminate against, any students who wish to conduct a meeting within that limited open forum on the basis of the religious, political, philosophical, or other content of the speech at such meetings."

Layperson translation: Public schools that receive federal funds and that allow non-curriculum-related clubs to form and meet at the school cannot bar some groups to form based on their religious, political, philosophical, or other content.

Importance to LGBT: Has prevented school officials hostile to LGBT people from refusing to allow the formation of gay-straight alliances.

Title IX of the Education Amendments of 1972
Commonly referred to as "Title IX"
U.S. Code Title 20, Chapter 38, Section 1681
20 U.S.C. § 1681(a).

The text: "No person in the United States shall, on the basis of sex, be excluded from participation in, be denied the benefits of, or be subjected to discrimination under any educational program or activity receiving federal financial assistance."

Layperson translation: No one shall be excluded on the basis of sex from participating in any educational program that receives federal funding. (Its name, Title IX, refers to its position in the original legislation, and it is today still identified by that designation.)

Importance to LGBT: When the Department of Education released revised regulations for the enforcement of Title IX in 1997, it explicitly noted that the law could be used to address antigay harassment that creates a sexually hostile environment in the schools. It has also been interpreted by some courts to protect students who do not conform to sex stereotypes.

Family Educational Rights and Privacy Act (FERPA)
U.S. Code Title 20, Chapter 31, Subchapter III, Part 4,
    Section 1232g
20 U.S.C. § 1232g

The text: "No funds shall be made available under any applicable program to any educational agency or institution which has a policy of denying, or which effectively prevents, the parents of students who are or have been in attendance at a school of such agency or at such institution, as the case may be, the right to inspect and review the education records of their children."

Layperson translation: Public schools that receive federal funding must allow parents of students the right to see their children's records.

Importance to LGBT: If your school records include any indication of your being gay, such as your membership in a gay group, your parents may have access to this information.

Appendix F
Finding Legal Help

Lambda Legal Defense and Education Fund

Lambda Legal is the largest, oldest national gay legal group in the country. It has its headquarters in New York City and regional offices in Atlanta, Chicago, Dallas, and Los Angeles. Lambda files lawsuits in cases that can establish positive legal precedents that will affect LGBT people and people with HIV. It operates a Legal Help Desk to provide legal information and/or referrals to other organizations, as well as advice on how to find a lawyer.

Web site: lambdalegal.org

E-mail: legalhelpdesk@lambdalegal.org

Phone: New York	(212) 809-8585
Atlanta	(404) 897-1880
Chicago	(312) 663-4413
Dallas	(214) 219-8585
Los Angeles	(213) 382-7600

American Civil Liberties Union—Lesbian, Gay, Bisexual, Transgender & AIDS Rights Project

The ACLU is one of the oldest, largest, and best-known national civil rights organizations in the country, and its Lesbian and Gay Rights Project has been at the forefront of gay civil rights litigation. Like Lambda, the ACLU focuses on filing lawsuits that can benefit many people. The organization is headquartered in New York.

Web site: aclu.org

E-mail: getequal@aclu.org

Phone: (212) 549-2627

Gay & Lesbian Advocates & Defenders (GLAD)

While smaller in size and geographical coverage, GLAD is one of the most respected gay civil rights groups in the country. It focuses its work in the six New England states of Massachusetts, Vermont, New Hampshire, Maine, Rhode Island, and Connecticut. Like Lambda and the ACLU, it files lawsuits based on the likelihood of their benefiting many people. It operates a Legal InfoLine to provide information and referrals. The organization is based in Boston.

Web site: glad.org
E-mail: gladlaw@glad.org
Phone: (617) 426-1350

National Center for Lesbian Rights (NCLR)

Despite what its name suggests, the National Center for Lesbian Rights works on litigation, public policy, and public education issues for lesbians, gay men, bisexuals, and transgender people. It's one of the oldest gay legal organizations in the country—thirty years old as of 2007—and recently became bicoastal, setting up regional offices in Florida and Washington, D.C., to help its national headquarters in California. It has been a leader in pressing for the rights of youth and transgender people.

Web site: nclrights.org
E-mail: info@nclrights.org
Phone: San Francisco   (415) 392-6257
       Florida   (727) 490-4260
       Washington   (202) 737-0012

Appendix G
Organizations for LGBT Youth

There are numerous national, state, and local organizations that focus on helping LGBT youth or that have programs focusing on youth. These are just a few that work with LGBT young people and that provide referrals to other groups and resources.

Gay, Lesbian, & Straight Education Network (GLSEN)

A national nonprofit organization focused on ensuring safe schools for all students, GLSEN promotes an annual "Day of Silence" to draw attention to discrimination and harassment against LGBT students. Its Web site provides information on how to organize gay-straight alliances, publishes reports documenting the prevalence of harassment against LGBT students, and provides numerous other resources to help students improve the climate for learning in their schools.
Web site: glsen.org
E-mail: glsen@glsen.org
Phone: (212) 727-0135

National Youth Advocacy Coalition

A national organization that advocates for LGBT young people, the National Youth Advocacy Coalition provides information and referrals to local help lines, support groups, LGBT health centers, and legal resources. Based in Washington, D.C., it also provides support for youth who do not identify as LGBT but are "questioning" their sexual identity.
Web site: nyacyouth.org
E-mail: nyac@nyacyouth.org
Phone: (800) 541-6922, ext. 12

Safe Schools Coalition

A national coalition of organizations that focus on or have programs focusing on helping LGBT youth by improving the climate for them at school. Its Web site has links to many of these organizations, including Parents, Families and Friends of Lesbians and Gays and Scouting for All. It operates a Crisis Phone at (877) SAFE-SAFE. And it provides information and referrals on a wide variety of topics of interest to young LGBT people, including school laws and policies. It is based in Seattle.

Web site: safeschoolscoalition.org

E-mail: questions@safeschoolscoalition.org

Phone: (206) 632-0662 x 49

Appendix H
Four Landmark Cases in LGBT Law

Here are brief case summaries of four court opinions that have had enormous significance in legal challenges brought by LGBT people.

1. *Lawrence v. Texas*

Decision by:	U.S. Supreme Court
Citation:	539 U.S. 558
Date:	June 26, 2003
Parties:	John Lawrence and Tyron Garner v. State of Texas
Issue:	Enforcement of law prohibiting consensual same-sex sodomy in privacy
Result:	Sodomy law found unconstitutional
Grounds:	Fourteenth Amendment right to liberty in U.S. Constitution

Excerpt: "Liberty presumes an autonomy of self that includes freedom of thought, belief, expression, and certain intimate conduct.... [Sodomy] statutes do seek to control a personal relationship that, whether or not entitled to formal recognition in the law, is within the liberty of persons to choose without being punished as criminals. This, as a general rule, should counsel against attempts by the State, or a court, to define the meaning of the relationship or to set its boundaries absent injury to a person or abuse of an institution the law protects. It suffices for us to acknowledge that adults may choose to enter upon this relationship in the confines of their homes and their own private lives and still retain their dignity as free persons. When sexuality finds overt expression in intimate conduct with another person, the conduct can be but one element in a personal bond that is more enduring. The liberty protected by the Constitution allows homosexual persons the right to make this choice."

Additional notes: You'll notice that the Court appears to be signaling that it may not be inclined to find that same-sex couples are entitled to marriage licenses. Nevertheless, in striking down state sodomy laws, the court eliminated a long-standing legal relegation of gay men and lesbians in many states to a status as presumed criminals—a status used against them in many contexts to justify discrimination against them.

2. *Goodridge v. Department of Public Health*

Decision by: Massachusetts Supreme Judicial Court
Citation: 798 N.E.2d 941
Date: November 18, 2003
Parties: Julie and Hillary Goodridge and others v. State Dept. of Public Health
Issue: Refusal to issue marriage licenses to same-sex couples
Result: Refusal declared unconstitutional
Grounds: Equal protection in the state constitution

Excerpt: "Marriage is a vital social institution. The exclusive commitment of two individuals to each other nurtures love and mutual support; it brings stability to our society. For those who choose to marry, and for their children, marriage provides an abundance of legal, financial, and social benefits. In return it imposes weighty legal, financial, and social obligations. The question before us is whether, consistent with the Massachusetts Constitution, the Commonwealth may deny the protections, benefits, and obligations conferred by civil marriage to two individuals of the same sex who wish to marry. We conclude that it may not. The Massachusetts Constitution affirms the dignity and equality of all individuals. It forbids the creation of second-class citizens. In reaching our conclusion we have given full deference to the arguments made by the Commonwealth. But it has failed to identify any constitutionally adequate reason for denying civil marriage to same-sex couples."

Additional notes: Although gay couples have been quietly seeking equal rights in marriage since 1971, none succeeded until this lawsuit. The result of this decision led not only to the issuance of the first legally valid marriage licenses for same-sex couples in the United States, but also triggered an unprecedented discussion of gays and marriage in the public at large, in the 2004 presidential election, and in the LGBT community itself. The success also triggered a political backlash, prompting legislators and voters in many states to approve measures aimed at banning both same-sex marriage licensing in their states and to ban recognition of marriage licenses of same-sex couples from other states. Subsequent litigation extended the right of same-sex couples in Rhode Island to obtain marriage licenses in Massachusetts, but Rhode Island has yet to determine whether it will recognize these licenses.

3. *Romer v. Evans*

Decision by: U.S. Supreme Court
Citation: 517 U.S. 620
Date: May 20, 1996
Parties: Roy Romer, as Governor of Colorado v. Richard Evans, a Colorado gay activist
Issue: Voter-approved Amendment 2 to eliminate any legal protections based on sexual orientation.
Result: Measure declared unconstitutional
Grounds: Fourteenth Amendment right to equal protection in U.S. Constitution

Excerpt: "We cannot accept the view that Amendment 2's prohibition on specific legal protections does no more than deprive homosexuals of special rights. To the contrary, the amendment imposes a special disability upon those persons alone. Homosexuals are forbidden the safeguards that others enjoy or may seek without constraint.... These are protections taken for granted by most people either because they already have them or do not need them; these are protections against exclusion from an almost limitless number of transactions and endeavors that constitute ordinary civic life in a free society.... The amendment has the peculiar property of imposing a broad and undifferentiated disability on a single named group.... Its sheer breadth is so discontinuous with the reasons offered for it that the amendment seems inexplicable by anything but animus toward the class that it affects; it lacks a rational relationship to legitimate state interests.... We must conclude that Amendment 2 classifies homosexuals not to further a proper legislative end but to make them unequal to everyone else. This Colorado cannot do. A State cannot so deem a class of persons a stranger to its laws."

Additional notes: By striking down Colorado's antigay Amendment 2, the decision put an end—for a while—to a national campaign to pass such ballot measures around the country. The opinion would also seem to signal that laws could no longer be based on animus toward LGBT people.

4. *Hopkins v. Price Waterhouse*

Decision by:	U.S. Supreme Court
Citation:	490 U.S. 228
Date:	May 1, 1989
Parties:	Price Waterhouse v. Ann Hopkins
Issue:	Whether employer can discriminate based on gender stereotypes
Result:	Practice ruled a form of sex discrimination
Grounds:	Title VII of the Civil Rights Act of 1964, prohibiting sex discrimination

Excerpt: "In order to improve her chances for partnership, [a supervisor] advised, Hopkins should 'walk more femininely, talk more femininely, dress more femininely, wear make-up, have her hair styled, and wear jewelry.'... In the specific context of sex stereotyping, an employer who acts on the basis of a belief that a woman cannot be aggressive, or that she must not be, has acted on the basis of gender.... We are beyond the day when an employer could evaluate employees by assuming or insisting that they matched the stereotype associated with their group."

Additional notes: The decision that sex discrimination includes insisting that an employee look and act in a manner associated with a gender stereotype meant that the federal civil rights law's prohibition of discrimination in employment could be extended to afford some protection for LGBT people, who often do not meet the expectations of gender stereotypes.

Glossary

administrative law. A law created by a governmental department or agency to explain how a statute will be implemented or enforced. Also known as a regulation.

age of consent. Age, set by state law, at which a person is considered capable of voluntarily consenting to sex.

age of majority. The age at which you are considered an adult under law. This age is set by state law and most states set it at eighteen (There are four exceptions—nineteen in Alabama and Nebraska, twenty-one in Mississippi and Pennsylvania.) Until you reach this age, your parents or legal guardians are responsible for your care, empowered to make numerous decisions on your behalf, and entitled, with some exceptions, to see your medical and school records. Once you turn the age of majority, you are automatically considered legally emancipated.

bisexual. Person who is attracted sexually to both men and women.

circuit court. In the federal court system, an intermediate court of appeal where a party who has lost a lawsuit in the court of entry can ask that a specific constitutional issue or issues be reexamined. In a state court system, the initial court where a lawsuit is heard.

complaint. A lawsuit.

district court. In the federal court system or some state court systems, the court where a lawsuit is initially heard.

due process. Procedures required by law and/or a requirement that such procedures are administered uniformly and fairly.

emancipated minor. A person who has not reached the age of majority but who has obtained the legal right to be considered an adult. This can be done either through a court order, by getting married, or by joining the military. (Requirements for emancipation vary from state to state, as does age requirements for marriage. The minimum age for joining the military is seventeen, but requires parental consent.)

equal protection. A constitutional guarantee that people in similar legal situations will be treated similarly under the law.

gay, lesbian. Person whose sexual attraction is mostly or exclusively oriented to a person of the same sex and who self-identifies as a member of a community of other gay men and lesbians.

guardian ad litem. An adult appointed by a judge to protect the interests of a minor.

heterosexual. Person who has sex with a person of the other sex.

homosexual. Person who has sex with a person of the same sex.

minor. Person who has not yet reached the age of majority.

moot. No longer posing an active legal issue.

next friend. Legal adult who stands in for a minor in a lawsuit brought on behalf of the minor. This person is usually a parent or other relative and is not considered a party to the lawsuit.

regulation. A law created by a governmental department or agency to explain how a statute will be implemented or enforced. Also known as "administrative law."

sodomy. Historically, sexual acts that do not lead to procreation. Defined legally by state law but generally include anal intercourse and oral sex.

statute. A law created by a legislative body, such as Congress or a state legislature.

transgender person. A person who lives and/or experiences life as a person of the gender other than the one with which his or her physical body is typically associated. The term used to describe a wide variety of persons, including those who have had surgery to change from one physical gender to the other, those who are contemplating such surgery, those who don't want such surgery but who dress in a way so as to appear to be the gender other than their physical attributes are ascribed to, and people who only occasionally dress to appear to be the other gender.

unemancipated minor. A person who is younger than the age of majority and who is still under the care of his or her parents or guardians.

Notes

1. It's Your Fight

1. For a list of laws state by state, go to the Web site of the Juvenile Law Center (www .jlc.org) and click on "Fact Sheets" and then "Age Requirements for Various Activities." That will take you to a page where you can look up the "age of majority" law in your state.
2. *California Codes, Family Code*, sections 7120–7123.
3. *The Crime Control Act of 1990* (42 U.S.C. 5779) includes a provision added in 2003 called "Suzanne's Law," which increased from eighteen to twenty-one the age below which a missing individual is considered to be a "child" whose status law enforcement agencies must report to the National Crime Information Center. The law enables law-enforcement agencies to begin searching for such persons immediately upon receiving a report; no waiting period is required.
4. *The 26th Amendment: Pathway to Participation* (Alexandria, VA: Close Up Foundation, 2001), p. 3.
5. As casually as these terms are employed in conversation today, it's important to note that "lesbian" and "gay" are very specific terms that mean more than "homosexual." As discussed in a later chapter, "homosexual" refers to someone who has sex with a person of the same sex. "Lesbian" refers to a woman who is sexually attracted to women and who may or may not have had sex with a woman but who voluntarily identifies herself as being part of that group. "Gay" refers to a man—or a woman— who is sexually attracted to people of the same sex, who may or may not have had sex with a person of the same sex but who voluntarily identifies as being part of that group. "Bisexual" refers to a man or a woman who is sexually attracted to both men and women and who may or may not have had sex with a man or a woman. A bisexual may or may not identify as being part of a group of lesbians or gays. A transgender person is someone who was born with the physical body of one gender but who identifies more strongly with the other.

    The acronym LGBT, which stands for "lesbian, gay, bisexual, and transgender," is frequently used in conversation by members of the LGBT community and will be used in this book to make sentences less cumbersome.
6. "Sexual minority" is a term often used to refer collectively to people who identify themselves as lesbian, gay, bisexual, or transgender. Estimates vary as to what percentage of the general population identifies as part of a sexual minority. Statistics attempting to gauge the size of the LGBT community are discussed in Chapter 2.
7. Human Rights Watch, "Women's Rights," www.hrw.org/women.
8. U.S. Department of State, Office of International Religious Freedom, *Annual Report on International Religious Freedom*, 2005, www.state.gov/g/drl/irf/.

9. The *Communications Decency Act* of 1996 was part of an omnibus *Telecommunications Act of 1996*.

10. *Reno v. American Civil Liberties Union*, 521 U.S. 844 (1997).

11. Harris Interactive and the Gay, Lesbian, & Straight Education Network, *From Teasing to Torment: School Climate in America, A Survey of Students and Teachers* (New York: GLSEN, 2005).

12. Quoted in Lambda Legal Defense and Education Fund, "Lambda Legal Sees Rise in Hostility toward Gay Youth Since Election, Expands Its Education Campaign to 'Hot Spots' in Missouri, Utah, Alabama, Iowa, Texas," press release, December 9, 2004.

13. Ibid.

14. Joseph G. Kosciw and Elizabeth M. Diaz, *The 2005 National School Climate Survey: The Experiences of Lesbian, Gay, Bisexual, and Transgender Youth in Our Nation's Schools* (New York: GLSEN, 2006).

15. *Hatred in the Hallways: Violence and Discrimination against Lesbian, Gay, Bisexual and Transgender Students in U.S. Schools* (New York: Human Rights Watch, May 2001), introduction, paragraph 1.

2. You're a Sex Symbol

1. In common parlance, people often use the terms "sex" and "gender" interchangeably when discussing whether someone is a male or female. But in certain contexts, the words refer to different things. In discussions about whether a person is male or female, "sex" refers to genitalia and "gender" refers to their behavioral, cultural, or psychological characteristics.

2. While "opposite sex" is a commonly used term, many find the phrase to be inaccurate. To use color as an analogy, the difference between men and women is less like that between the opposites black and white than that between blue and red. A more apt term may be the "other sex."

3. *National Youth Survey 2004* (Minneapolis: Center for Democracy and Citizenship, Council for Excellence in Government; College Park, Md.: Center for Information and Research on Civic Learning and Engagement [CIRCLE], February 2004).

4. National Center for Health Statistics, U.S. Centers for Disease Control, *Sexual Behavior and Selected Health Measures: Men and Women 15–44 Years of Age, United States, 2002*. Based on data from the National Survey of Family Growth, the report found that 10 percent of the 4,928 men and 8 percent of the 7,643 women surveyed had never had sex. *Advance Data from Vital and Health Statistics* 362 (September 15, 2005).

5. 539 U.S. 558 (2003).

6. For an explanation and discussion of how age-of-consent laws affect youth, see Chapter 7.

7. The 2002 *National Survey of Family Growth*, conducted by the National Center for Health Statistics, U.S. Centers for Disease Control and Prevention, looked at the respondents' same-sex partners in the past twelve months and at any point in their life-

times. Averaging the percentages for both men and women who had had partners in the previous twelve months, they accounted for 5.2 percent of the population in the nation's twelve largest metropolitan areas, but only 2.4 percent of nonmetropolitan areas. Other breakdowns showed even greater differences—for instance, 4.8 percent of men in the largest metropolitan areas had had a same-sex partner in the previous twelve months, whereas only 1.5 percent of men in nonmetropolitan areas had.

8. According to the fact sheet "U.S. Teen Sexual Activity" published in January 2005 by the Kaiser Family Foundation, recent studies found that the "median age at first intercourse is 16.9 years for boys and 17.4 years for girls."

9. Alfred C. Kinsey et al., *Sexual Behavior in the Human Male* (Philadelphia: Saunders, 1948) and *Sexual Behavior in the Human Female* (Philadelphia: Saunders, 1953).

10. Personal interview with the author.

11. Transgender people include a wide variety of persons—those who have had surgery to change from one physical gender to the other, those who are contemplating such surgery, and those who adopt the dress and behavior more associated with the other sex.

12. Jessica Xavier, "A Primer by Transgender Nation" (Transgendered Nation and Washington, D.C., Parents, Families, and Friends of Lesbians and Gays). One of a series of handouts available through the PFLAG-Talk/TGS-PFLAG virtual library (www .critpath.org/pflag-talk/tgprimer).

13. *Sexual Behavior and Selected Health Measures: Men and Women 15–44 Years of Age, United States, 2002.* Although the questions were asked face-to-face, respondents answered by typing their answers privately into a laptop computer.

14. The question posed to women was different from that posed to men. Women were asked about "sexual experience" in general; men were asked specifically about "oral or anal sex."

15. Looking only at the responses from fifteen-to-nineteen-year-olds, the survey found 5.8 percent of females had had both male and female partners. Among twenty-to-twenty-four-year-olds, 4.8 percent of females had had both male and female partners.

16. For a good overview of this work, see Dean Hamer and Peter Copeland, *The Science of Desire: The Search for the Gay Gene and the Biology of Behavior* (New York: Simon & Schuster, 1994). The book discusses Hamer's study, at the National Cancer Institute, which found a distinctive pattern in one region of the X chromosome of more than 80 percent of study participants, gay men who had a gay brother.

3. The Evolution of Difference

1. Exodus 21:20–21 says that if a man beats his servant to death, the man must be punished. But if the servant survives the beating a day or two, the man shall not be punished because the servant "is his money." Leviticus 19:27 commands that people not shave or cut their hair. Leviticus 11 would seem to prohibit the eating of pork and all shellfish.

2. John Boswell, *Christianity, Social Tolerance, and Homosexuality: Gay People in West-*

ern Europe from the Beginning of the Christian Era to the Fourteenth Century (London and Chicago: University of Chicago Press, 1980).

3. From "The Church and the Homosexual: An Historical Perspective," an address to the Fourth Biennial International Convention of Dignity, a gay Catholic group, in 1979.

4. In his discussion of the origins of homosexuality, Brent Pickett explains that there were "general strictures against same-sex *eros*" in parts of Ionia, a series of coastal cities south of Lesbos. Pickett, "Homosexuality," in *The Stanford Encyclopedia of Philosophy* (electronic resource), edited by Edward N. Zalta (fall 2002), http://plato .stanford.edu/.

5. Ibid.

6. Theo van der Meer, "The Persecutions of Sodomites in Eighteenth-Century Amsterdam: Changing Perceptions of Sodomy," in *The Pursuit of Sodomy: Male Homosexuality in Renaissance and Enlightenment Europe*, edited by Kent Gerard and Gert Hekma (New York: Haworth, 1989), pp. 263–307.

7. *Journal of Homosexuality* 16, nos. 1 and 2 (1988), special issue.

8. *American Journal of Psychiatry* 107 (1951): 787.

9. In *Lawrence v. Texas,* the majority opinion noted that the institute "justified its decision on three grounds: (1) The prohibitions undermined respect for the law by penalizing conduct many people engaged in; (2) the statutes regulated private conduct not harmful to others; and (3) the laws were arbitrarily enforced and thus invited the danger of blackmail."

10. Dr. Evelyn Hooker, "Final Report of the National Institute of Mental Health Task Force on Homosexuality," better known as the Hooker Report, was first published in *ONE Institute Quarterly: Homophile Studies* 8, no. 22 (1970), edited by W. Dorr Legg and published by the Educational Division of ONE, Inc.

11. In 1973 the APA reclassified homosexuality from a "sexual orientation disturbance" to a "sexual deviation" disorder. The new designation was considered necessary to guide psychiatrists working with people who experienced same-sex attraction but who were either "disturbed by, in conflict with, or wish[ed] to change their sexual orientation." Otherwise, the APA diagnostic manual listed homosexuality as simply "one form of sexual behavior." Eventually, the manual came to remove any suggestion that homosexuality constituted a disorder.

12. Personal interview with author, 1989.

13. According to historian Bob Summersgill, the Idaho legislature adopted the model code only to reject it after learning that it included the repeal of its sodomy laws.

14. In *Lawrence v. Texas,* the majority decision, written by Justice Anthony Kennedy, noted that, "it was not until the 1970s that any State singled out same-sex relations for criminal prosecution, and only nine States [had] done so."

15. *Doe v. Commonwealth's Attorney for the City of Richmond*, 403 F.Supp. 1199 (ED Va.1975).

16. Sodomy laws were also used to prosecute alleged rapists when the evidence was not sufficient to convict them on the more serious charge.

17. 478 U.S. 186 (1986).
18. Abby Rubenfeld, "With *Hardwick* Lost, What Now?" *Washington Blade*, July 4, 1986, p. 6.
19. *Commonwealth v. Wasson*, 842 S.W. 2d 487 (Ky. 1992).
20. 517 U.S. 620 (1996).

4. The Least You Need to Know

1. *Sterling v. Borough of Minersville*, 232 F.3d 190 (3rd Cir. 2000).
2. The ruling was made in *Griswold v. Connecticut*, 381 U.S. 479 (1965), a case that asked whether the government of Connecticut could enforce a state law that prohibited providing access to "any drug, medicinal article or instrument for the purpose of preventing conception."
3. In *Griswold* the Court said that a married couple had a privacy right to make such a decision, and in *Eisenstadt v. Baird*, 405 U.S. 438 (1972), it said that unmarried couples had a privacy right to do so.
4. *Roe v. Wade*, 410 U.S. 113 (1973), in which the Court ruled that a woman has a right to decide whether or not to have an abortion.
5. *Whalen v. Roe*, 429 U.S. 589 (1977).
6. The Second Circuit (covering New York, Connecticut, and Vermont) has ruled that "the excruciatingly private and intimate nature of transsexualism, for persons who wish to preserve privacy in the matter, is really beyond debate" (*Powell v. Scrivner*, 175 F .3d 107, 111 [1999]). The Sixth Circuit (covering Michigan, Ohio, Kentucky, and Tennessee) ruled that "our sexuality and choices about sex . . . are interests of an intimate nature which define significant portions of our personhood. Publicly revealing information regarding these interests exposes an aspect of our lives that we regard as highly personal and private" (*Bloch v. Ribar*, 156 F.3d 673 [1998]). The Ninth Circuit (covering California, Oregon, Washington, Arizona, Montana, Idaho, Nevada, Alaska, and Hawaii) issued a similar ruling in *Thorne v. City of El Segundo*, 726 F.2d 459 (1980). The Tenth Circuit (covering Colorado, Kansas, New Mexico, Oklahoma, Utah, and Wyoming) ruled that "minors possess a right to informational privacy concerning personal sexual matters," in *Eastwood v. Dept. of Corrections*, 846 F.2d 627 (1998).
7. *Walls v. City of Petersburg*, 895 F.2d 188 (4th Cir. 1999).

5. It's Alive!

1. Family Research Council, introduction to the brochure *Judicial Activism and the Threat to the Constitution*, www.frc.org/get.cfm?i=BC05F01.
2. The South's Army of Northern Virginia was surrendered to the Union on April 9, 1865. The Thirteenth Amendment, to abolish slavery, was ratified on December 6, 1865. The Fourteenth Amendment, guaranteeing that all former slaves would have the equal rights of citizenship, was not ratified until July 9, 1868. And the Fifteenth

Amendment, guaranteeing them the right to vote, was not ratified until February 3, 1870.

3. Anthony made this comment in a speech delivered on numerous occasions following her conviction for voting in a presidential election prior to the Nineteenth Amendment's ratification. See *Elizabeth Cady Stanton, Susan B. Anthony: Correspondence, Writings, Speeches,* edited by Ellen C. DuBois (New York: Shocken, 1981).

6. Law: The Mother of All Arts

1. Michigan and New York State laws require that companies rent to qualified drivers between the ages of eighteen and twenty-five, but New York allows companies to charge younger drivers a surcharge of as much as one hundred dollars per day. Some car rental companies have recently started extending their services to drivers between the ages of twenty-one and twenty-five.

2. The *National Minimum Drinking Age Act* of 1984 does not prohibit you from *drinking* alcoholic beverages if you're under twenty-one. It prohibits you from purchasing them or possessing them in public except in certain circumstances—such as when you're with your parents, at a religious service, or at a private club.

3. For a discussion of important exceptions to the medical-treatment rule, see Chapter 11.

4. *Policy concerning Homosexuality in the Armed Forces,* 10 U.S.C. Section 654. The quote is contained in the policy as a congressional finding.

5. C. Dixon Osburn, executive director of the Servicemembers Legal Defense Network, stated, in an e-mail correspondence with author, that "the armed forces have never produced one shred of evidence to back up their claims that lesbian, gay or bisexual service members disrupt unit cohesion, good order, discipline or morale."

6. 1 U.S.C. § 7 (1997) and 28 U.S.C. § 1738C (1997).

7. Statement by Florida state senator Curtis Peterson in introducing legislation to ban gays from adopting. See ACLU petition to U.S. Supreme Court in *Steven Lofton v. Secretary of the Florida Department of Children and Families,* filed October 1, 2004. The Supreme Court refused to review the lower court decision, which upheld the policy.

8. For more information on how to look up laws, see Appendix A.

9. The "Don't Ask, Don't Tell" policy provides for only very specific circumstances under which a gay or bisexual person can serve in the military.

10. Personal interview with author.

11. As this book was being written, efforts were under way to have more states consider such bans.

12. In summer 2006, the U.S. Senate and House failed—for the second time—to muster enough votes to pass a bill that sought to amend the U.S. Constitution to limit the definition of marriage to only straight couples. However, supporters of the bill have vowed to submit it again in the future.

13. There are exceptions. Some state constitutions include a provision that local govern-

ments may not promise more rights to citizens than guaranteed by the state constitution.

14. In *Pacific Employers v. Industrial Accident*, 306 U.S. 493 (1939), the U.S. Supreme Court ruled that the full faith and credit clause does not go so far as to require one state to be compelled "to substitute the statutes of other states for its own statutes dealing with a subject matter concerning which it is competent to legislate," especially when those laws conflict.

15. As of the writing of this book, Massachusetts is the only state that grants marriage licenses to same-sex couples.

16. E-mail correspondence with author.

7. Sex: Legal and Not

1. National Center for Health Statistics, U.S. Centers for Disease Control, *Sexual Behavior and Selected Health Measures: Men and Women 15–44 Years of Age, United States, 2002*.

2. The examples of how sodomy laws were used against openly LGBT people in the workforce are many. One of the more well-known examples was Mica England, a lesbian who was rejected for a job with the Dallas Police Department. England, in 1994, won a settlement that included an agreement to change the department's hiring practices. See "Lesbian Settles Suit for Bias in Dallas," *New York Times*, September 16, 1994.

    In Virginia, just months before sodomy laws were struck down, the legislature voted against reappointing a judge to a state circuit court bench because a female employee had accused her of sexual harassment. The sexual harassment charge had been dismissed as baseless, but a state legislator convinced other legislators that the allegation meant the judge was gay and, therefore, that she had violated the state law against sodomy.

    With respect to child custody, these cases, too, are many. One example occurred in Virginia, where a court cited the state's sodomy law in denying custody to a lesbian mother, Sharon Bottoms. *Bottoms v. Bottoms*, 249 Va. 410, 457 S.E. 2d 102 (1995).

    Auburn University in Alabama rejected an LGBT campus group's request for funding, citing a state law that prohibited the college from spending funds to support a group that "promotes a lifestyle or actions prohibited by the sodomy and sexual misconduct laws." A federal judge ruled that the law violated the U.S. Constitution's First Amendment. See *Gay, Lesbian, Bisexual Alliance v. Sessions*, 917 F.Supp. 1548 (MDAla.1996).

    Finally, an editorial in the *Idaho Press Tribune*, July 10, 2000, noted that the state legislature had tried to censor public television programs that discussed homosexuality in a positive or neutral light. "Clinging to an Idaho statute against sodomy," said the editorial, "self-appointed morality enforcers contend that nonjudgmental programming about homosexual issues promotes a practice that violates Idaho law."

3. *State v. Matthew Limon*, 32 Kan. App. 2d 369 (2004).

4. *Commonwealth of Virginia v. Joel Singson.*

5. "Consent" is defined by state law. For instance, in Alabama, a sexual act is considered to have taken place without consent if there was "forcible compulsion," an "incapacity to consent," or sexual abuse whereby the victim did not "expressly or impliedly acquiesce" to the act; a person is considered incapable of giving consent if he or she is younger than sixteen, mentally "defective" or mentally incapacitated, or physically helpless. See *Alabama Criminal Code,* Title 13A, Article 4, Section 13A-6-70.

6. In West Virginia, Section 61-8-4 of the state code prohibits "any persons, not married to each other" from "lewdly and lasciviously associate[ing] and cohabit[ing] together." In five other states, similar laws apply to "any [unmarried] man and woman," so it's not clear whether such laws could be used against same-sex couples. (See *Florida Statute* 798.02, *Michigan Compiled Laws* 750.335, *Mississippi Code,* 97-29-1, *North Carolina General Statutes* 8-57, and *North Dakota Criminal Code* 12.1-20-10.) In Kansas, having sex with someone who is married to someone else is prohibited by K.S.A. 21-3507.

7. Section 2451.11 Public display of offensive sexual material, under the Penal Code of the *New York State Consolidated Laws.*

8. 720 ILCS 5/11-7.

9. *Nevada Revised Statutes* 201.190; 201.354; and 41.370.

10. *Alaska Statutes,* Title 11.41.427.

11. Lambda Legal Defense and Education Fund, *Little Black Book,* available on the organization's Web site, in English and Spanish.

12. The *Commonwealth of Virginia v. Joel Singson* conviction was upheld by an appeals court, and the state supreme court refused Singson's appeal.

13. Code of Virginia, Section 18.2-63; California Penal Code, Section 261.5; Iowa Code 72.5.

14. At promotetruth.org, simply click on "laws" and then look up your state's age-of-consent law. The Web site also includes other state laws of interest, including laws concerning harassment, the reporting of child abuse, and parental consent for abortions.

15. Each state defines "statutory rape" in its own way, but generally speaking the term is used to describe sexual intercourse with any person below the age of consent.

16. *Missouri Revised Statutes,* 566.034.

17. Some court briefs on Matthew's behalf pointed out that his sexual partner was "almost fifteen"; however, technically speaking, the law is based on the person's actual age.

18. *Kansas Statutes* 21–3503.

19. *Kansas Statutes* 21–3522.

20. *Kansas Statutes* 21–3505. Even after the U.S. Supreme Court struck down all state sodomy laws in June 2003, a Kansas appeals court refused to hear Matthew's appeal to have the charge against him dismissed. He was eventually released after the Kansas Supreme Court reviewed the case, but he had already spent more than five years in jail.

8. Pleading the First

1. Web site of the Legal Information Institute, Cornell Law School, www.law.cornell.edu/.
2. This tactic doesn't work when the attorneys are working "pro bono"—or for free. And civil rights law groups, such as the ACLU and Lambda Legal Defense and Education Fund, typically provide their services without cost to the plaintiffs. However, these groups don't take every worthy case. They generally take only those cases that are establishing some point of law that affects a large number of people.
3. Rendering something "moot" means the issue is no longer active and viable. For instance, if an apartment manager refuses to rent an apartment to you for some discriminatory reason and you file a lawsuit, and then the apartment building accidentally burns to the ground and will not be rebuilt, then your lawsuit will likely be considered moot.
4. "Federal Judge Rules That High Schools Cannot Out Lesbian and Gay Students," ACLU press release, December 1, 2005.
5. *Schenck v. U.S.,* 249 U.S. 47 (1919).
6. "NYC Reggae Concert Canceled after Protests of Anti-Gay Lyrics," Associated Press, July 12, 2006.
7. *LaStaysha Myers v. Jeff Thornsberry,* United States District Court for the Western District of Missouri, Case No. 05–5042.
8. "ACLU Secures Promise from Missouri High School to Stop Censoring Student's Gay-Supportive T-Shirts," ACLU press release, June 23, 2005.
9. *Tinker v. Des Moines School District,* 393 U.S. 503 (1969).
10. "Speaking Out with Your T-Shirt," ACLU press release, January 30, 2006.
11. See U.S. Supreme Court decision in *Bethel School District No. 403 v. Fraser,* 478 U.S. 675 (1986).
12. "Speaking Out with Your T-Shirt."
13. "No Prom for Boy in Dress," Associated Press, May 25, 2006.
14. The National Center for Lesbian Rights is a national LGBT legal resource center; Equality Florida is a statewide education and advocacy group for LGBT people.
15. Under the U.S. Code, this law appears within Title 20, which deals with education, and runs from Section 1681, which addresses discrimination, through 1688, concerning abortion.
16. Quote is from the ACLU brief to the Eleventh Circuit in support of Nikki Youngblood's appeal and refers to *Price Waterhouse v. Hopkins,* 490 U.S. 228 (1989). In *Price Waterhouse,* the accounting firm had rejected a female employee for a promotion because leaders at the firm felt she was too masculine and that she should "walk more femininely, talk more femininely, dress more femininely, wear make-up, have her hair styled, and wear jewelry." The Supreme Court found this to be in violation of the Civil Rights Act's Title VII.
17. *Price Waterhouse v. Hopkins,* 490 US 228 (1989).
18. "GenderPAC National News Interviews Nikki Youngblood," July 1, 2002. Gender PAC Web site.

9. The Powers of Assembly

1. *NAACP v. Alabama,* 357 U.S. 449 (1958).

2. The most significant difference by far is that most LGBT people can—unlike most racial minorities—hide the characteristic that makes them most vulnerable to discrimination. This ability provides only *individuals* with an ability to escape discrimination in *some* circumstances and, for most people, the price of doing so exacts a large measure of self-respect.

3. *Norton v. Macy,* 417 F.2d 1161, 1164, U.S. Court of Appeals for the District of Columbia (1969).

4. Randy Shilts, "How the FBI Spied on Gays: 20 Years of Secret Files," *San Francisco Chronicle,* September 21, 1989, p. A1.

5. The Servicemembers Legal Defense Network (SLDN), a national legal services and watchdog organization concerned about the U.S. military's discriminatory policies against LGBT people, obtained documents from the DOD in 2006 indicating that the department had conducted surveillance on student groups and protests of its anti-gay policies at universities in California, New Jersey, and Connecticut. The surveillance documents, available on SLDN's Web site, state that the reports were compiled to alert the military to "potential terrorist activity" or "force protection issues." They include the contents of e-mail correspondence, and the protests are referred to as "suspicious activities."

6. The county was named for David T. White, who helped in its formation. Coincidentally, 95 percent of the county's population is white.

7. From complaint filed by the ACLU in U.S. District Court for Northern District of Georgia, Gainesville Division, February 27, 2006. *White County High School PRIDE v. White County School District.*

8. See *U.S. Code,* Title 20 (Education), Sections 4071–74.

9. *Palmer High School Gay/Straight Alliance v. Colorado Springs School District No. 11,* No. 03–2535 (D.Colo. Mar. 30, 2005).

10. William C. O'Kelley of the U.S. District Court for the Northern District of Georgia, Gainesville Division, in a decision released July 14, 2006, in *White County High School Pride v. White County School District.*

11. The Parental Equal Access to Information Act was approved by the Georgia legislature as part of a larger education bill (Senate Bill 413) in March 2006.

12. See "Memorandum in Support of Motion to Reopen Case," *Boyd County High School Gay Straight Alliance v. Board of Education, U.S. District Court Eastern District of Kentucky, Ashland Division,* July 5, 2005.

13. The gay-straight alliance at Lake City High School in Coeur d'Alene, Idaho, appears to have overcome this obstacle for some students by naming itself the "Human Rights Club" and defining its purpose as addressing "human rights challenges locally and around the world."

14. In a 1970 decision, *re Theodore William Cox,* the California Supreme Court ruled "that the act specifies particular kinds of discrimination—color, race, religion, an-

cestry, and national origin—serves as illustrative, rather than restrictive, indicia of the type of conduct condemned." 3 C3d 205. Then, in 1982, a state appeals court ruled, in *Hubert v. Williams*, 133 Cal.App.3d Supp. 1, 5, that the act's prohibition on arbitrary discrimination extended to gay people.

15. *Timothy Curran v. Mount Diablo Council of the Boy Scouts of America*, Supreme Court of California, March 23, 1998.

16. In 1998 President Bill Clinton signed an executive order prohibiting discrimination based on sexual orientation in federal employment. However, under President George W. Bush, the office that would enforce that order has indicated an unwillingness to do so.

17. The states are California, Connecticut, Hawaii, Illinois, Maine, Maryland, Massachusetts, Minnesota, New Hampshire, New Jersey, New Mexico, New York, Rhode Island, Vermont, Washington, and Wisconsin.

18. As discussed elsewhere in this book, there are individual federal laws that provide some protection in *specific* instances, such as when a gay-straight alliance wants to meet on school grounds or the discrimination is based on sex stereotypes.

19. *Boy Scouts of America v. James Dale*, 530 U.S. 640 (2000).

20. *Saxe v. State College Area School District*, 240 F. 3d 200 (3rd Circuit, 2001). In a decision led by current U.S. Supreme Court justice Samuel Alito, a three-judge panel ruled that the policy did violate the U.S. Constitution's guarantee of free speech, but the panel's chief concern seemed to be that the school policy, as written, was overbroad (it prohibited "any unwelcome verbal...conduct which offends...an individual because of" various personal characteristics) and so vague as to proscribe behavior or speech even outside of school.

21. In several lawsuits filed by the Christian Legal Society, for instance, the religious campus groups assert that membership is limited to students willing to sign a "Statement of Faith" that says that "engaging in or advocating any sexual conduct, whether heterosexual or homosexual, outside the confines of traditional marriage is immoral."

22. *Christian Legal Society v. James Walker*, U.S. Court of Appeals for the Seventh Circuit, July 10, 2006.

10. When Your Life Is On the Line

1. Sometimes you'll hear attorneys talk about the right to due process under the Fifth Amendment. It is promised in both places. In the Fifth, it is considered a promise of the federal government; in the Fourteenth, it is a promise to be honored by the states as well.

2. *Jamie Nabozny v. Mary Podlesny et al.*, U.S. Court of Appeals for the Seventh Circuit, July 31, 1996, 92 F.3d 446. On the due-process claim, the court said that the schools have no "duty to protect" students. "Duty to protect" is a specialized legal term for a legal obligation one party has to protect another party from danger. The obligation is usually limited to situations in which the government has a "special relationship" with a person such that the person is necessarily dependent on the government for

protection (for instance, when police have a person in custody or a court has committed a person to a psychiatric institution). In 1989 the U.S. Supreme Court ruled that the government has no "duty to protect" citizens from "private actors." ("The affirmative duty to protect arises not from the State's knowledge of the individual's predicament or from its expressions of intent to help him, but from the limitation which it has imposed on his freedom to act on his own behalf." *DeShaney v. Winnebago City,* 489 U.S. 189.) The federal appeals panel in the *Nabozny* case relied on the *DeShaney* decision in deciding that the school had no "special relationship" with any student that required it to protect the student from other students. However, the court indicated that there had been evidence that school officials had "created a risk of harm, or exacerbated an existing one."

3. Harris Interactive and the Gay, Lesbian, & Straight Education Network, *From Teasing to Torment: School Climate in America: A Survey of Students and Teachers* (New York: GLSEN, 2005), p. 1.

4. *The 2003 National School Climate Survey: The School-Related Experiences of Our Nation's Lesbian, Gay, Bisexual, and Transgender Youth.* The results of the survey, conducted by the Gay, Lesbian, & Straight Education Network, is available online at www.glsen.org.

5. FBI, *Hate Crime Statistics 2005,* November 2006.

6. Interestingly, the West Chester University Web site includes a chart listing various bias-related crime categories for the years 2003 and 2004 but shows zero crimes in each. The FBI report for 2004 shows 12 gay-related hate crimes and 3 religion-related hate crimes for the university.

7. Tim Gay, "Are the Kids Alright? Harassment Is Still a Problem," *Villager* 73, no. 7 (June 16–22, 2004).

8. From *Henkle v. Ross Gregory et al.* complaint filed by Lambda Legal Defense and Education Fund in the U.S. District Court for Nevada.

9. "Derek Henkle: Survivor of School Violence in Reno, Nevada," available on Web site of Lambda Legal Defense and Education Fund.

10. 42 U.S.C. § 1983.

11. *Oncale v. Sundowner,* 523 U.S. 75 (1998).

12. John Koopman, "Ex-Student Hopes Settlement Will Stop Anti-Gay Attacks," *San Francisco Chronicle,* August 29, 2002.

13. Mark Bixler, "Cherokee Residents Mourn Loss of Teen," *Atlanta Journal and Constitution,* November 5, 1998.

14. *Official Code of Georgia Annotated,* Chapter 2, Title 20, 751.4 and 751.5.

15. For a list of these states, see Appendix D.

16. 20 U.S.C 7133.

17. National Center for Education Statistics, U.S. Department of Education, and Bureau of Justice Statistics, U.S. Department of Justice, "Indicator 11: Students' Reports of Being Called Hate-Related Words and Seeing Hate-Related Graffiti," *Indicators of School Crime and Safety: 2005.* Available from either agency's Web site.

18. U.S. Department of Education Office for Civil Rights and National Association of At-

torneys General, Bias Crimes Task Force, *Protecting Students from Harassment and Hate Crime* (Washington, D.C., January 1999).

19. According to the FBI's *Hate Crime Statistics 2005,* only 13.5 percent of reported hate crimes motivated by sexual orientation took place at schools or colleges.

20. Ronald Smothers, "Teenage Girl Fatally Stabbed at a Bus Stop In Newark," *New York Times,* May 13, 2003, p. 8. And see Keith Boykin, "Sakia Gunn Remembered," keithboykin.com.

21. "Homicide Victim's Mom Leads Protest," *Courier-Journal,* Louisville, Kentucky, June 12, 2006.

22. Andy Newman, "Defendant Gets 25 Years for Beating Gay Man," *New York Times,* April 25, 2006, page 3.

23. Currently, federal law allows for increased penalties for hate crimes based on sexual orientation only if the crime constitutes a "federal crime," such as one committed on federal property or crossing state lines. 18 U.S.C. 245.

24. Hate Crime Statistics Act, 28 U.S.C. 534.

25. Federal Bureau of Investigation, U.S. Department of Justice, *Crime in the United States 2004, Uniform Crime Reports,* November 14, 2005.

26. FBI, *Hate Crime Statistics 2005.*

27. David Buckel, *Stopping Anti-Gay Abuse of Students in Public Schools: A Legal Perspective* (New York: Lambda Legal Defense and Education Fund, 1998). Available at Lambda's Web site by clicking on "Issues," "Youth and Schools," "Resources," and then the publication's title.

28. U.S. Department of Education Office for Civil Rights and National Association of Attorneys General, Bias Crimes Task Force, *Protecting Students from Harassment and Hate Crime.*

29. Buckel, *Stopping Anti-Gay Abuse.*

30. Based on *Preventing Hate Crime: What We Can Do,* a publication of the Crime and Violence Prevention Center of the California Attorney General's Office.

31. "General Safety Tips—Help Prevent an Attack," New York City Gay & Lesbian Anti-Violence Project Web site (www.avp.org).

11. Protecting Your Privacy

1. Anthony R. D'Augelli et al., "Parents' Awareness of Lesbian, Gay, and Bisexual Youths' Sexual Orientation," *Journal of Marriage and Family* 67 (May 2005): 474–82. The survey involved interviews with 528 youths in New York City and environs; 307 were raised by either two "opposite-gender" parents or a single parent. And of these 307, 293 were included in the final survey sample. (Fourteen teens with "opposite gender" parents were dropped because there was a difference in awareness between their two parents—in other words, one parent was understood to be aware of their child's sexual orientation while the other was not.) The responses were worded in this very specific way because some teens were raised by a single parent and some by two

parents. For the 293 teens, there were 413 parents total—288 mothers or maternal figures (grandmother, stepmother, etc.) and 125 fathers or paternal figures.

2. The Kinsey Scale, developed by Alfred Kinsey (see Chapter 2) from his extensive interviews and research, shows a person's sexual orientation as tending to fall somewhere along a continuum from zero to six, and as potentially changing over time. A zero represents someone who is "exclusively heterosexual with no homosexual" experience and 6 represents someone who is "exclusively homosexual."

3. The "Boyhood Gender Conformity Scale" was developed by Stewart Hockenberry and Robert Billingham at Indiana University's Department of Applied Health Science. A "Feminine Gender Identity Scale" was developed by Kurt Freund et al. (two men and one woman) at the University of Toronto.

4. D'Augelli, "Parents' Awareness," p. 479.

5. Ibid., p. 481.

6. National Public Radio, Kaiser Family Foundation, Kennedy School of Government, *Sex Education in America: General Public/Parents Survey* (January 2004), available at the Web site of the Kaiser Family Foundation, www.kff.org.

7. Cathy Schoen, Karen Davis, and Catherine DesRoches, *The Commonwealth Fund Survey of the Health of Adolescent Girls* (New York: Commonwealth Fund, 1997) and *The Health of Adolescent Boys: Commonwealth Fund Survey Findings* (New York: Commonwealth Fund, 1998).

8. Web site of Patient Privacy Rights Foundation, www.patientprivacyrights.org.

9. Public Law 104, 191.

10. Section 164.502 Uses and disclosures of protected health information: general rules, (3)(i) Implementation specification: unemancipated minors. "HIPAA Administrative Simplification Regulation Text," U.S. Department of Health and Human Services, Office of Civil Rights, 45 CFR Parts 160, 162, and 164 (Unofficial Version, as amended through February 16, 2006), p. 49.

11. Ibid., p. 50.

12. "Standards for Privacy of Individually Identifiable Health Information," Final Privacy Rule Preamble, Office of the Assistant Secretary for Planning and Evaluation, U.S. Department of Health and Human Services, *Federal Register* 65, no. 250 (December 28, 2000).

13. American Medical Association Policy no. 140.

14. According to the CDC, as of December 31, 2002, eight states (California, Hawaii, Illinois, Kentucky, Maryland, Massachusetts, Rhode Island, and Vermont), the District of Columbia, and Puerto Rico had a code-based system for collecting information on people with HIV infection. Five states (Delaware, Maine, Montana, Oregon, and Washington) had a system in which they initially collected names and, after any necessary public health follow-up, converted the names into number codes. Connecticut and New Hampshire allow cases to be reported by name or code. All other states, said the CDC, have laws or regulations requiring confidential reporting by name of both adults and adolescents. CDC, "Technical Notes: Surveillance of HIV Infection (not AIDS)," July 12, 2006.

15. "Student Spots Patient Records On-Line," United Press International, February 10, 1999.

16. Kenneth R. Gosselin, "Careless Disposal of Records Imperils Privacy Paper Chase," *Hartford Courant*, May 14, 1999, p. D1.

17. *Jerric D. Ballensky v. Jan Marie Flattum-Riemers, M.D.*, North Dakota Supreme Court, 2006 ND 127, June 5, 2006.

18. "Confidential Health Care for Adolescents: Position Paper of the Society for Adolescent Medicine," *Journal of Adolescent Health* 35, no. 2 (2004): 160–167.

19. Ibid.

20. *Texas Family Code*, Chapter 32, Subchapter A, Section 32–003.

21. 20 U.S.C. Section 1232g; 34 CFR Part 99.

22. 740 Illinois Compiled Statutes 110.

Index

Adams, Michael, 9
age of consent, 60–61, 137
age of majority, 2, 60, 101, 137
Amendment 2, Colorado, 30, 48, 134–135
amendments, U.S. Constitution: First,
  63–75, 77–78, 80, 83, 85, 120, 121;
  Fifth, 149; Thirteenth, 143n; Four-
  teenth, 76, 79, 87, 121, 130, 134, 143n;
  Fifteenth, 143n; Nineteenth, 38;
  Twenty-Sixth, 38, 139
American Academy of Family Physicians,
  107
American Civil Liberties Union (ACLU),
  62, 64, 69, 70–72, 74, 116, 128, 147n,
  148n
American Law Institute, 26–27, 118
American Medical Association (AMA),
  99, 104
American Psychiatric Association (APA),
  27, 119, 142n
American Psychiatric Institute, 27
Anthony, Susan B., 39, 144n
Ashland School District, 88
association, freedom of, 10, 63, 75, 84
Auburn University, 145n

Baker v. Nelson, 119
Ballensky v. Flattum-Riemers, 153n
ballot initiative, 48
Belluardo, Josh, 91, 92
Bernardino of Siena, 24
Bethel School District No. 403 v. Fraser,
  147n
Bill of Rights, 34, 36, 39
Blair Jr., Timothy, 94
Bloch v. Ribar, 143n
Boswell, John, 22, 141n
Bottoms v. Bottoms, 145n

Bowers v. Hardwick, 29–30, 53, 55, 120–121
Boy Scouts of America, 82–85, 121
Boy Scouts v. Dale, 84–85, 149n
*Boyd County High School Gay Straight
  Alliance v. Board of Education,* 148n
Brennan, Justice William, 120
Brown University, 89
Bryant, Anita, 119
bullying, 92–93, 123
Bush, George W., 149n

Centers for Disease Control and Preven-
  tion, U.S. (CDC), 17, 105
Chhun, Crystal, 66
Christian Legal Society, 85, 149n
Christian Legal Society v. James Walker,
  149n
*Christianity, Social Tolerance, and
  Homosexuality* (Boswell), 141n
Circuit Court of Appeals, U.S.: First, 51;
  Second, 143n; Third, 34–35; Fifth, 120;
  Sixth, 143n; Seventh, 85, 87, 149n;
  Eighth, 120; Eleventh, 74, 147n
Civil Rights Act of 1964, U.S., 74, 90, 121,
  125, 135, 147n
Civil Service Commission, U.S., 77, 119
Civil War, 38, 87, 116, 143n
Clevenger, Cliff, 117
Clinton, Bill, 121, 149n
Close Up Foundation, 3
clothing, 44–45, 72–73. *See also* T-shirt
  messages
clubs, 10, 45, 63, 78, 81, 126
Commonwealth of Virginia v. Joel Singson,
  146n
Commonwealth v. Wasson, 143n
Communications Decency Act of 1996,
  U.S., 140n